CELIBACY

and the

Crisis of Faith

Dietrich von Hildebrand

CELIBACY

and the

Crisis of Faith

Franciscan Herald Press

Celibacy and the Crisis of Faith by Dietrich von Hildebrand was originally published as *Zoelibat und Glabuenskrise* by Josef Habbel, Regensburg, West Germany, 1971. Translated into English by Dr. John Crosby. Copyright © 1971 by Franciscan Herald Press, 1434 West 51st Street, Chicago, Illinois 60609. Library of Congress Catalog Card Number: 72-155851; SBN: 8199-0428-7. Made in the United States of America.

~~~~~~

NIHIL OBSTAT:
  Mark Hegener O.F.M.
  Censor Deputatus

IMPRIMATUR:
  Rt. Rev. Msgr. Francis W. Byrne
  Vicar General, Archdiocese of Chicago

August 30, 1971

IN JESU CHRISTO DILECTAE AMICAE
KARLA MERTENS
BENEFICIORUM MEMOR

Foreword

When we consider what the Second Vatican Council[1] as well as the magnificent encyclical of our Holy Father Pope Paul VI, *Sacerdotalis Caelibatus,* has to say about obligatory celibacy for priests in the Western Church, it may seem superfluous to want to say anything further on this subject.

But it is perhaps not unimportant, at a time when so many bishops, priests, and laymen are attacking celibacy, to hear the voice of a married layman who has written so much about the grandeur and beauty of marriage.

Furthermore, the attacks against obligatory celibacy have not relented after the encyclical, as one would expect, but have rather increased.

This obstinate blindness and this complete lack of understanding for the encyclical is however less astonishing when we consider what grave errors have penetrated into many levels of the Church.

NOTES

1. "For these reasons, which are based on the mystery of the Church and her mission, celibacy was at first recom-

mended to priests. Then, in the Latin Church, it was imposed by law on all who were to be promoted to sacred orders. This legislation, to the extent that it concerns those who are destined for the priesthood, this most holy Synod again approves and confirms." "Presbyterorum Ordinis," para. 16.

Contents

Introduction

Before dealing in detail with the question of whether obligatory celibacy for priests of the Western Church is desirable or undesirable, has a value or a disvalue, whether the state of the world somehow calls for the abolition of celibacy, or whether, on the contrary, it makes the celibacy of the priest especially necessary and important, we must deal briefly with the crisis which the so-called progressivists have provoked in the Church.

We must refer to certain fateful errors which are daily being propagated by theologians, priests and lay persons, and are gaining ground in the Church because most Catholic journals are in the hands of those propagating these errors, and these persons control much of the mass media and have a great deal of money at their disposal.

In my book, *The Trojan Horse in the City of God,* I have already dealt in considerable detail with many of these errors.

Nevertheless, it is necessary to refer briefly here again to some of the errors mentioned there, and also to point out others which I did not go into in my book. The reasons put forward for the abolition of celibacy must be viewed in the light of the mentality so widespread in our time. We should never forget how easily people unconsciously make concessions to prevailing intellectual trends, and gradually become inured to the incompatibility of these trends with the true Christian faith.

The "Myth of Modern Man"

The first thesis which unfortunately impresses so many people is that man has changed so radically in this century that the revelation of Christ has to be presented to him in a new language and in a formulation different from that which the Church has been using for the last two thousand years. People are so naive that they do not realize that this thesis is completely arbitrary and that what it asserts as true is neither evident nor in any way scientifically founded. This myth of the "modern man" contains many equivocations, and it can mean very different things here.

As long as one only refers to the immense change in the external conditions of life brought about by the enormous technological development which has taken place, then one is referring to an indubitable fact. But this outward change has had no fundamental influence on man — on his essential nature, on the sources of his happiness, on the meaning of his life, on the metaphysical situation of man. And yet only some such fundamental change in man would have any bearing at all on his ability to understand the language in which the Church has been announcing the Gospel of Christ to mankind for thousands of years.

A modest knowledge of history and an unprejudiced view of it could not fail to convince anyone that the "modern man" who is radically different from the men of all other periods is a pure invention, or rather, a typical myth. I have dealt with this at length in my *Trojan Horse*.[1]

But even if one only means by "modern man" that the attitude towards many questions has changed, that a new mentality is prevalent today — a completely changed intellectual climate — it still remains a myth. Granted that the age is marked by certain widespread intellectual trends, it is nevertheless a typical inadmissible generalization to speak of "modern man" for that reason. There are many people today who are not stamped by this mentality, just as was the case in all ages. There is no such thing as the "modern man"; there are only widespread intellectual trends.[2]

A. The error that the essential nature of man is altered by a change in the spirit of the time.

Of course we find that the different epochs are characterized not only by different external conditions of life but also by a distinctive character, which enables us to speak of a Zeitgeist (spirit of the age).

Hence there is definitely sense in speaking of medieval man as distinguished from Renaissance man. It has been rightly emphasized, for example, that Dante was a medieval man, whereas Petrarch, though only 39 years younger, was a Renaissance man. It is quite clear in these cases that it is not a question of any radical alteration, of any change in human nature as such, any more than when one says of Molière that he is a typically French mind, of Schiller that he is typically German, or of Stifter that he is specifically Austrian.

In order to recognize clearly the mythological nature of the present-day phrase, "modern man," we must first go briefly into the real meaning of the distinction for instance between medieval and Renaissance man.

As we just said, different eras have a more or less distinctive character, just as different nations have. This character is expressed by certain widespread intellectual trends, by ideas, but even more by a certain *style* which affects everything from the high spiritual spheres of architecture and art down to the way of dressing. But the difference between these "spirits of the age" is a complementary rather than a contrary one. The spirit of the Renaissance, in as far as it is expressed in art and in the style of life, although it differs greatly from the medieval spirit, does not differ in the sense of an antithesis but rather in the sense of a complementary difference. For in the sphere of *culture,* truth is not the theme as it is in philosophy and religion, the theme is rather beauty, originality, intellectual richness; thus a deep difference between two authentic cultures has not got the character of a mutually exclusive opposition such as that between false philosophical theories and authentic philosophical truths. In the latter case only one can be true. In the case of cultural periods one can of course speak of higher and lower — they have not all the same value — but they do not differ in a contradictory way.

Epochs differ not only in the value of their culture but also in that one epoch has a much more strongly marked character of its own than another. Or a given period may be so chaotic that no clear spirit of the age and no style of its own can be discerned in it.

Hence one must not confuse the character of a period of culture with the mere historical and sociological prevalence of certain ideologies. This kind of historical and sociological "reality" of certain ideas at a particular moment and in a particular country does not suffice to give that time a definite character of its own. For these trends of a given time are often the artificial products of one or several persons who succeed in demagogically attracting a great following. These artificial ideologies and their historical-sociological reality often have a very brief life and can be replaced at any moment by trends in the opposite direction. We should surely have learned that from

Hitler's "Reich of a Thousand Years," which lasted only twelve years.

But the chief thing to understand in this context is that the authentic "style" of a period never touches the deepest roots of man and of his nature. There is a certain specific quality of the men who are typical of the spirit of their age, and this justifies us in contrasting the medieval and the Renaissance man. It is an incomparably less deep and decisive difference than that, say, between a stupid, ungifted, or even morally low person on the one hand, and a genius or a person of noble moral character on the other. This applies even in art: the difference between an insignificant, conventional medieval church and a Chartres Cathedral is much greater and more decisive than the difference between the exterior of Chartres and that of St. Peter's in Rome. But whereas in the sphere of art all great works, although timeless, are nevertheless deeply colored by the spirit of the age, this is very much less the case with the individual man.

We repeat: man, in his ontological structure — in his character of *imago Dei* — of spiritual person — is not changed by the spirit of the time. But even the decisive qualitative differences of man lie beyond the reach of the spirit of the age. It is certain peculiarities in the attitude towards life, in the role which certain interests play, in the style of life, and in the *Lebensgefühl,* which justify our speaking of a medieval man and of a Renaissance man.

Hence, the first great error in the myth of modern man is the belief that the spirit of the age radically changes or could change man.

B. The confusion of a prevailing ideology with an unalterable fate.

But as soon as one takes the spirit of the age understood in the idoleogical sense, that is, in the sense of a predominant philosophy such as rationalism, materialism or empiricism, to be an unalterable and natural stage in a process of intellectual evolution, an unfolding of the Hegelian Weltgeist (world-spirit), one falls into a second error, and one not only lives in an illusion but also takes an attitude which is completely incompatible with the Christian revelation. For one is then putting a Hegelian Weltgeist in the place of God, and adaptation to a given stage of development becomes the decisive measure, instead of what has been revealed to us through the Old and the New Testament as true, good and pleasing to God.

As soon as one makes history the source of revelation instead of the Gospels and the traditional teaching of the Church and thus tries to adapt even the content of the deposit of the Catholic faith to the alleged stage of development, one can no longer in honesty call oneself a Catholic, or even a Christian; for this is unambiguous apostacy from Christ.

These contemporary intellectual trends are not the

natural and inevitable product of the evolution of history, or of the Hegelian Weltgeist, but are to a large extent the result of a vast propaganda and of a certain kind of education.

It is a huge error to assume that, because these trends are nurtured by non-religious and anti-religious elements, the Church is obliged to present the Christian revelation in a new language to the Catholics of 1970, as they allegedly no longer understand the traditional language, or it no longer "interests" them. A close look at history shows clearly that there have been at all times intellectual movements in which the spirit of the world made eyes blind and ears deaf to the Gospel of Christ.[3]

In spite of this the voice of Christ still reached many souls; the language of the Church was still understood by her children, and in every age since the Reformation there have been many great converts such as Newman or Maritain. One must of course know the intellectual trends of the times, and welcome and "baptize" what is good in them. But, as John XXIII said, the Church must imprint her seal on every age and every nation, not the other way around. The Church must above all fight against everything which is incompatible with the spirit of Christ; she must make no compromise and must not formulate the Christian message in a way completely inadequate to its real substance and thus falsify it.

To sum up: we maintain emphatically that the

theory that man has changed completely in his essential nature in the twentieth century is not only an arbitrary, unproven assertion, but one that is clearly false and in no way corresponds to the facts. History, on which people take their stand so readily today, shows this clearly. The fact that there are currents of thought which are characteristic of the present age in no way justifies assuming that everyone in this age is stamped by them. That is a pure invention of the sociologists. In reality, the differences among people in one and the same period are incomparably greater and more significant than the differences that result from different historical periods and f r o m changes in the external conditions of life.[4]

Finally, these trends of the time do not represent a given state of things fully withdrawn from our control. Today many people maintain emphatically that the radius of human influence has been vastly extended. Things which formerly were regarded as unalterable natural conditions can now be influenced and altered thanks to inventions of all kinds. But here, where there never was any question of a "fact of nature" but of something which formerly was not regarded as unalterable and beyond our influence, this spirit of the age is suddenly represented as an unalterable reality.

All this is implied in the slogan of the modern man and it is devoid of any scientific basis.

The error that the "form" of Revelation has to be adapted to each historical era.

But it is also important to realize what a great error it is to think that the form in which the Catholic faith is presented, must be adapted — without alteration of the content — to each succeeding age. In the first place, the separation of content and form is something very questionable. There is after all a deep inner relation between content and form. A religious truth demands an adequate form. We shall come right back to this point, which is also eminently important for the liturgy.

But apart from this connection between content and form, where does the difference for instance in a dogma between mere formulation and content begin? Granted that in principle one and the same truth can be differently formulated, is there not an extraordinarily great danger that a falsification of the truth could slip in when it is being reformulated?

This danger is all the greater, the more mysterious and weighty the truth is. Have not many heretics tried to introduce their heretical doctrines by what seemed to be merely new formulations of a dogma?

The new catechisms — the various ones for children in America, the French Catechism, as well as the incomparably more subtle Dutch Catechism — are clear examples of how the content of divine revelation can be radically falsified under the label of a more understandable formulation for the present day.

A. The sacred, and the holiness of God — desacralization, and hatred of God.

Simply the desacralization of the formulation, of the language, falsifies the content. Religion and the sacred are inseparably bound together. This is not only true for the Catholic Church but as well for the orthodox church and all forms of a truly believing Protestantism.[5] It is also true for the orthodox Jews, for Islam, even for the Oriental religions such as Brahmanism and Tibetan Buddhism. The sacred is a fundamental element of the religious, and whoever wants to eliminate it from the Church has lost the true faith. Such a person says, full of hatred: "Away with the sacred; it is time that we eliminate this superstition." But in fact he also means, "Away with the supernatural." For the sacred, as we just said, is a fundamental element of the religious — even of religions which contain many errors. The "supernatural," which is only found in the Christian Revelation, includes incomparably more than the sacred. But it is the source and the soul of the truly sacred, it is the sun whose rays are somehow present in every religion and constitute its sacredness. To want to desacralize the Church means inevitably not only to falsify her substance, not only to destroy the very attitude of faith; hatred of the sacred is in reality hatred of God.

For if the sacred is despised, so will the holy in the full sense of the word, as it is revealed to us in the

Old and New Testament. In the holy we find an ultimate interpenetration of absolute moral goodness and
the sacred, as this is revealed to us in Leviticus, in the
prophets, but in a completely new way in the holy
humanity of Christ, the Epiphany of God.

**B. "Kindness" instead of mercy — "earthly messias"
instead of Christ.**

The new translations of sacred scripture, especially
those in use in the vernacular Mass in America, show
in a fearful way how this desacralization not only
destroys an adequate religious atmosphere (this atmosphere is of the greatest religious importance and
it is a great lapsus mentis to dismiss all concern for
it as aestheticism), but also undermines the substance
of the content of faith, that is, of the revelation of
the Old and New Testament. The grave falsification
is apparent when for instance *misericordia* is translated as kindness instead of mercy (I pointed this
out in my *Trojan Horse*), or when Christ is replaced
by Messias.[6] Mercy is the basic message of the divine
revelation in the Old and New Testament. Here our
total dependence on God's mercy is expressed. The
glory of the infinite, incomprehensible love of God,
the deep relation between mercy and redemption on
the one hand and mercy and the repentance of man
on the other — all this is obscured by the word
"kindness"; and it is obscured not simply because of
an inability to translate well (although there is that
too), but rather because of the intention to make the

message of Christ harmless, to adapt it to the merely natural, to desacralize it, to remove from it the call to metanoia.

C. The form which is required by the content; distortions of the content simply by changing the appropriate form.

But even if we prescind from the danger of falsifying the content of the deposit of the Catholic faith by some new formulation which is supposed to make it more accessible to the mythical "modern man," the very idea of separating content and form is very doubtful. For there is a certain form which the content requires. The tone of the language in which something is expressed can either correspond to or contradict the spirit of the content. Even if the content remains unchanged, still a style of language contrary to the spirit of the content falsifies the content. If one were to translate the content of the Bagavad Ghita into the style of Bert Brecht, the content would clearly be distorted; if one were to formulate the content of the Koran into the language of a modern journalist, the content would similarly be distorted. The translations of the liturgy of the holy Mass and especially of the readings have shown us in the last four years in a fearful way: the attempt to translate these into a "new language" in order to make them more living and contemporary has indisputably led to a distortion of the sacred atmosphere and thus indirectly of the spirit of the content.

A new language is called for by many, particularly for the liturgy, on the grounds that pastoral considerations require it. One says, in comparison to the pastoral question what does it matter whether the Missale Romanum of St. Pius V and the Gregorian Chant are a more adequate expression of the content than the present liturgy — to be concerned with this is aestheticism. The decisive thing is whether it is better understood and absorbed by modern men. True charity must put pastoral considerations in first place.

Pastoral considerations and the types of "attraction," ranging from the _fascinans_ of God to the complete opposite of this.

Despite the great emphasis today on pastoral considerations, the nature of the pastoral is completely misunderstood by many. One often hears: We must form the liturgy in such a way that it becomes more attractive to the young, that church attendance becomes greater. But the decisive question here is: what does "attract" mean? Man has many levels, some superficial, some deep, and there are many ways of appealing to him, some legitimate, others illegitimate. A good comedian appeals to a legitimate but relatively superficial level in us. Great art attracts the man who has a sense for it, and this attraction is not only legitimate but good. Such art clearly appeals to a much deeper level in us than the charming comedian.

Pornography appeals to an illegitimate level in us, to an impure, base sensuality. Similar though more harmless is the appeal of trivial, sentimental music for certain persons; such music appeals to an illegitimate level in them. The appeal of jazz is also illegitimate; it usually appeals to a certain chaotic, subhuman dynamism, to a "letting oneself go" and being dragged into an animal vitality.

This should suffice to show that the mere formal power of attraction tells us nothing as long as we do not know *why* something attracts us, to what level it appeals in us. An abyss separates the evil, base attraction or "siren song" of all temptations, from the good and noble attraction of goods which embody genuine values. Our very way of speaking expresses this: the attractive power of those things which appeal to our concupiscence and our pride is called temptation, whereas it would clearly be meaningless to say of a magnificent landscape or a great work of art that it "tempts" us in deeply moving us and elevating us. Similarly the attraction of a person whom we deeply love is utterly different from, for example, the attraction of taking revenge on another.

Not only is that which attracts us different in such cases, but the formal nature of the attraction is in each case different. The attraction of the holiness and beauty of Jesus is unique and incomparable — it is the power of attraction of God, of which St. Augustine says, "parum voluntate, etiam voluptate trahimur,"[7] and of which the saints have spoken of in a marvelous way. The word of God, His holy truth, the Epiphany of God in the sacred humanity of Jesus, all these appeal to the deepest level of our soul and draw us up in a way which cannot be compared even with the attraction of the highest natural goods such as truth, beauty, and love.

Now it is absurd to think that men can be brought to God, that more persons can be brought into church by dropping the sacred language of the Church and introducing a kind of liturgy which appeals to quite peripheral and sometimes even to illegitimate levels in man. In this way men cannot be led to God, one rather counteracts the true power of attraction of the holy. One cannot even use this false attraction as a temporary means of attracting men to God.

The story is told of Don Bosco that as a young man he was once saying the rosary with some others, when suddenly a trumpet sounded from the street announcing the arrival of a tight-rope walker. Everyone ran out of the church to see him perform. Don Bosco went with them and took part in the acrobatic tricks of the circus. He performed them so much better than the professional acrobat that the crowd broke out in enthusiasm and began loudly applauding him. Then he said to them: why don't we go back to church and continue praying. And those in the crowd who were so impressed by him went back with him and continued praying. In this case Don Bosco used the impression which his courage and skill made on the crowd, in order to draw them away from the circus and bring them back to prayer. But he didn't make a circus out of the rosary; he didn't try to blend the atmosphere of the church with elements of the circus, for these appeal to a completely different level in man. He simply used the good name which he made for himself by his skill, in order to bring men back to prayer. But he did not make prayer "attractive" by drawing it into a circus atmosphere, with the result that the authentic, sacred attraction of the church would be replaced by a harmless, sensational attraction.

This story shows us clearly the equivocation committed in saying that we can use all things which possess a legitimate power of attraction, in order to win men for God. This using can mean that we use these legitimate profane means to win men for God, to persuade them to come to church so that there they might be exposed to the radically different, sacred atmosphere. But this using can also mean that we so distort the atmosphere of the liturgy itself, that it appeals to low, peripheral levels in man and that it deceives men as to the nature and meaning of the worship of God.

The confusion of love with community

A widespread error today is the confusion of love with community. Although a deep unity is achieved in many types of love, such as love of parents for their children, love of children for their parents,

friendship, and above all marital love, we must nevertheless bear two facts in mind: there is a type of
community which involves no love, and there is a
type of love — love of neighbor — which neither
presupposes nor constitutes community in the full
sense.

We need hardly dwell on the fact that there are
many communities embracing many men who do not
even know one another, much less love one another
in any way. The state is a community embracing many
persons who do not know one another individually
and therefore cannot enter into personal relations with
one another. This also holds for nations, for humanity,
indeed for the holy Church. However deep the objective bond is uniting all members of the mystical body
of Christ, still this bond exists independent of whether
one Catholic knows another or even knows of his
existence, and of course independent of whether the
one Catholic has any personal love for the other. But
even when we prescind from the purely objective
unity in a community, we find that even the consciousness of community, the experience of being bound
with others does not presuppose any actualized relation among the individual members of the community.
The "we-consciousness," the consciousness of being
objectively bound with all the members of this community applies to all of them without our having to
know any of them. Potentially we have a relation to
every member of this community, and this relation

contains a kind of love according to the type of community in question. Everyone belonging to this community is somehow potentially included in our love. This is of course the case in an incomparably new way in the community represented by the holy Church.

The "we-community" is always grounded in a certain domain of goods with a certain theme. It is an objective domain of goods which objectively unites the members and which also in the experience of this unity plays a corresponding role. Thus the relation of the individual members to the community as a whole is decisive for the type and depth of the "we-community" among the members. In order for the citizens of the state to experience their unity, they must have a loyalty and even a love for the state. This is even more the case for a nation. But what we are saying takes on a completely new meaning in the case of the Church. Love for the Church plays of course a decisive role since it is grounded in the love for Christ. Love is here *more* required than in any other community. It is a completely new, incomparably deeper love which is here meaningfully required; also required is a unique devotion to the Church.

Now in the case of the Church there are many degrees of the consciousness of being bound with the other members. First of all the unity with others can be only potential, becoming actual only when we meet with other Catholics. And then the unity with these varies according to the depth of their faith, their love for Christ and his Church, their ardor, their awareness of the mystical body of Christ. In saying this I am prescinding from all other relations among Catholics, such as friendship, which may have preceded their meeting one another as Catholics, or may have developed after meeting one another in this way. I am thinking here of the unity which is expressed in the magnificent sentence of the liturgy: "Congregavit nos in unum Christi amor." As we said, there are many degrees of this unity which flows purely from the common love for Christ and his holy Church and from the consciousness of belonging together to the mystical body of Christ; this unity can vary in depth, intensity, and in the degree to which it is a source of happiness for those united; and of course our knowledge of the type and degree of the devotion of others plays a decisive role in determining our unity with them. But this unity can never embrace both Catholics and non-Catholics. However closely we can be bound to non-Catholics in friendship and love, however true it is that a quite different community based on love is entirely possible between Catholics and non-Catholics — nevertheless the unity which derives from objectively belonging to the mystical body of Christ is, according to the very meaning of this unity, necessarily confined to Catholics. All attempts to deny this in the name of ecumenism are attempts to achieve something nonsensical and intrinsically impossible.

There is another quite different and far less deep unity which embraces all believing Christians. But this community, this consciousness of unity is utterly different in kind — it is not the glorious communion of the mystical body of Christ — it is not the deep consciousness of unity which is grounded in faith in the entire deposit of Catholic faith and in the love for the holy Church, the bride of Christ. It is a much more abstract community and a much more "antithetical" one — that is, it is above all realized in the juxtaposition of Christians with non-Christians and even atheists. From this consciousness of unity we must again distinguish that which embraces all who believe in a personal God. The only unity we have with the rest of men is that grounded in the metaphysical community of mankind.

But the love of neighbor is simply independent of all community, of all "we-consciousness," of all consciousness of unity. Love of neighbor applies even to enemies of God, who reject all community with us. This love applies to everyone as soon as he becomes our neighbor, whatever his relation to us. This love does not strive for any community with the other, nor does it as such constitute any community. It only hopes for community with the other in the kingdom of Christ.

All love except for love of neighbor presupposes much more than merely being objectively united in a community. The value response to the beloved person which is contained in every love as well as the intentio unionis and intentio benevolentiae characteristic of every love — these presuppose a particular knowledge of the other person, an understanding of his special values, of the beauty and lovableness of his personality. None of this is presupposed for the we-consciousness of unity in an objective community. The element of love for the other members of the community (which varies according to the type of community) simply cannot be compared with love in the full sense. This element of love is a unity with the others which derives from a quite different source: from belonging to one and the same community. It is a kind of walking forward together, whether in a state, or a nation — only in the case of the holy Church is it a glorious unity in ultimate things. The important thing for us to understand is the difference between this objective community and the quite different community with others which is born of love.

Love of neighbor applies even to men with whom we should have no community

It would therefore be nonsense to argue from the fact that we ought to encounter everyone with Christian charity, to the fact that we ought to feel ourselves united in some kind of community with everyone. Every community, an objective we-community as well as the full personal unity grounded in love and a deep mutual understanding, has presuppositions different from those of charity.

True love of neighbor is above all inseparable from the love for Christ, the God-man, the Epiphany of God. Love of neighbor can only grow out of this love for Christ: the depth and breadth of our charity depends completely on the depth and breadth of our love for Christ. Only in loving the infinitely holy person of Christ can the love received at baptism develop in our soul. Only in the loving I-Thou relation with Jesus can He melt our hearts and bring out in our souls that holy goodness with which every true Christian approaches his neighbor and receives and embraces him. Charity also sees the value which every person as image of God possesses and which cannot be destroyed before the end of a person's life, that is, before his final decision for or against God — however repulsive and evil a man may be, however unlovable he has made himself. Thus no one is excluded from charity as long as he still lives and has not irrevocably turned away from God (of course it takes on a different character according to the person to whom it is directed). And so we clearly see how different the foundation for charity is from the foundation for all the various levels of community.

But we must go on to point out a further fact. Charity even extends to those men with whom we ought to have no community in the strict sense of community. If we take community in the sense of a "communicatio," of uniting together and forming a unity, then community is in certain cases not only not possible but not even right. I can and should have no community with evil. I should not act as if his moral wickedness were unimportant and as if I could ignore it and enter into a personal relation with him as I can and should with others. In speaking of the evil man I am definitely not thinking of the sinner. It would be terribly pharisaic of me to want to have nothing to do with a sinner, and this would be the very opposite of what Christ did. But the evil man in our sense here is not the weak man who keeps falling, the publican or the adulteress, but rather the deliberate enemy of God, the man who hates God and tries to poison the souls of others. Charity should be extended even to such a man, as we just saw, but we should have no community with him. This is expressed by St. John, the great apostle of love, when he writes: "If anyone comes to you and does not bring this doctrine, do not receive him into the house, or say to him, 'Welcome' " (2 Jn., 10).

The type of community in which we rejoice over being together with another, or where we just feel united with him in being and speaking with him, should not include the evil man, the enemy of God. We should not act as if it were unimportant to us that he works in the name of Satan. Many believe that this would be a striking sign of their lack of prejudice. They feel they are being "tolerant," they relish their generosity, and the way they can transcend the antithesis of good and evil. Recently the president of a

Jesuit college was criticized for inviting a Communist to an assembly of the college (the Communist was a cunning and notorious agent); he responded to this criticism by saying: "I don't hold anything against anybody." This is precisely the attitude which the apostle St. John condemns. This is unity achieved at the expense of God. It is a clear sign of indifference to God. Charity should of course extend even to the enemy of God — but I should have no community with him, I should never forget what an abyss separates me from him and that I cannot accept him as I might some unknown man.

Here we must make a further distinction. The community of which we are speaking here ranges from a deep consciousness of unity with for instance someone with whom we work, to a harmless, friendly encounter with another. To enter into any such community with the enemy of God would imply forgetting the barrier between us and him which his hatred of God has thrown up; we would be treating him as if he were a child of God and not the evil man of whom St. Paul says that we should not tolerate him in our community.

The situation is quite different when we approach an evil man in the hope of converting him. Our contact with him, which we undertake in order to perform this greatest act of charity toward him, does not have the character of entering into community with him; it does not involve ignoring his enmity with

God or sovereignly looking away from this. Just the opposite: the reason for our contact with him is precisely our deep grief over his enmity with God, our burning desire, flowing from charity, to lead him with the help of God to conversion. Far from putting aside his hostility to God and his errors, our whole purpose is, with the help of God, to change him from an enemy of God into a servant of God. Our contact with him is motivated by zeal for the glory of God, and love for God and neighbor. The community which we should not have with him is rather this "pseudo-generosity" at the expense of God which is the complete opposite of all charity, indeed it is deep indifference to the immortal soul of the evil man as well as to his eternal salvation. It is a bourgeois bonhomie, a cheap patronizing approach to the other. It is terrible to think that one often tries to justify this by appealing to the prayer of Christ, "ut unum sint," "that all may be one."

We have seen that charity as distinguished from community extends to every human being — even to the enemies of God. Charity presupposes much *more* in *our* soul than community does. It is only possible as the fruit of a burning love for Christ in which He melts our hearts and fills us with His holy love. But charity presupposes nothing in our neighbor, to whom we show charity. Communion with someone presupposes less in us, but much much more in the person with whom we enter into communion — and the deeper and more intimate the communion is, the more is presupposed in him.

Religious vitality and change

It is an illusion deeply rooted in human nature that it is a sign of being awake and alive when one changes existing things. To leave things as they are is regarded as a sign of inertness and ossification, whereas one is thought to be doing something important in intervening and changing. This is particularly the illusion of those who occupy a certain office or official position. But this overlooks that the protection and preservation of good things is a great sign of being awake and alive and is often a far more difficult task than changing and intervening. But the decisive error — the illusion of seeing in change as such a sign of being awake and being alive — comes from forgetting that the meaning and value of any change or preservation depends exclusively upon the things which are changed or preserved. If something is bad, then it should be changed if possible. If something is good and valuable, it is required of us that we strive to preserve it and keep it in existence. It is exclusively the object which determines whether changing and preserving is a sign of being awake and alive. As soon as I separate changing and preserving from the object changed or preserved, and see a value in changing as such or preserving as such, I commit a grave error.[9] The one decisive factor is the nature of the object, whether it is good or bad; it is only the adequate response to the nature of the object which is itself good and right and a sign of awakedness as opposed to inertly letting things take their course.

Of course it is not always a question of things having their value or disvalue in themselves, such as things which are good or evil, or truth, but rather of things having an indirect value or disvalue deriving from their effectiveness or appropriateness for a certain situation — such are customs, laws, institutions of all kinds. But even here we have to see that it is not necessarily a sign of true vitality to abolish existing laws, customs, and institutions; nor is it necessarily a sign of rigidity and unresponsiveness to preserve them. Only when the institutions or laws are no longer effective or appropriate to the situation is it a sign of life and awakedness to change them. When this however is not the case and a change is carried out without being required by the thing changed, then this change is no sign of life, it is rather a display of self-importance, it is irresponsible behavior motivated by the illusion that in changing one proves one's vitality and life. It is an act of Herostratic[10] pride; one wants to go down in history, or at least appear in the press. But usually the idea that one "accomplishes" something when one changes things (one confuses the feeling of being active with an objective achievement) is simply an illusion rooted in human nature.

The type of man who out of real indifference does fail to change things which should be changed at least does not live in any illusion, he is rather simply indifferent, irresponsible, lazy, or weak and fearful.

But the important thing is to see that preserving and protecting the good is a great task and often a much greater accomplishment than changing. It is a great error to see this required "activity" of preserving and protecting in the light of ossification and lack of life. This confusion is not only a mistake, it is also specifically stupid. It is the consequence of the naive illusion of seeing the highest manifestation of life and awakedness in change, and by posing the false alternative: if one does not change things, one has just mindlessly left everything as it was.

At the bottom of this illusion is the failure to understand that the primary mission of man lies not in creating but in cooperating. Man is primarily receptive (not passive!) in knowing, in being affected by values, in receiving the grace of God; and only on the basis of these receptive experiences is he capable of actively cooperating by giving the adequate response to the truth, to values, and above all to God. Such cooperation occurs in all value-responses when the will intervenes in the way required by the object; it also occurs in love, and in many other ways. We cannot further investigate here this general error which leads to an idolization of activity.

Today there is an orgy of "awakening" in the

Church. One constantly hears that the Council awakened the Church from her sleep, that new life is flowing into the Church, that it is time to change everything; one feels full of life in replacing faith in the revelation of Christ by all kinds of theories and defiling the glories of the liturgy by changes.

Here the illusion just discussed is present in a disastrous way. People believe they have awakened when in truth they are blinded. They take the loss of faith for an awakening simply because one often held the faith in a conventional way. But a true awakening does not consist in replacing the eternal, absolute truth of God by new human constructions, but rather in renewing our faith in the unchanged divine truth: that is, *we* must change by replacing a conventional faith with a fully awakened, living faith. We must not replace truth with error, we must not change the content of faith and fall into the illusion of thinking that, because we feel so alive in doing this, we are awakening to new life. In reality we have only fallen from a conventional faith in the truth into a completely unjustified enthusiasm for errors, or we have passed from faith to doubt. But doubt as to the truth, has nothing to do with awakening — it is rather a decline, a sickness. As to the liturgy, the true awakening consists in deepening ourselves in its glories, in opening our souls for its holy truth and its sacred atmosphere, for its mysteries, in letting ourselves be deeply moved by it — but this awakening does not consist in modernizing its content and form.

Let us understand that in speaking of the eternal youth of the Church we should above all think of the way in which her identity has been preserved through changing times and cultures. The great miracle of her indestructible life is that she has remained untarnished by all historical and cultural changes.

The "return" to the early Christian church

It is not only changing to accommodate "modern" man which can be wrong; it can be just as wrong to reintroduce early Christian forms.

Many believe that a return to the days of early Christianity is the way to true renewal. It is quite right that the true renewal does not just consist in changing many things in the Church; it rather consists above all in returning to the spirit of faith, of zeal, of heroism which filled the first Christians and which is expressed in the apostolic epistles and in the Acts of the Apostles.

This principle of renewal — returning to that first glorious time — should govern the renewal of the different religious orders, and in an analogous way should govern the renewal of many human relations, especially in marriage.

We must everywhere fight against the great danger of becoming inwardly deadened, of losing full awakedness, of falling into a slovenly self-abandon, of slipping into slavery to our habits and weaknesses. And if this fight is important with regard to great natural goods (such as marriage), then it is much more important with regard to our religious lives.

Now this returning to our origins, to the moment when God deeply touched our soul, while it is an essential part of all true renewal, must not be confused with a return to all details of the original state of things. It is a return to the original awakedness, to the original burning zeal which is required — not necessarily to the original structures.

When we are dealing with things which, as in the parable of the mustard seed, reach their full form through a process of organic development, it is by no means renewal to cut away all organic growth and to try to make the mustard tree look once again like the mustard seed. In the case of the mustard tree this is clearly impossible — but heretics of all kinds have repeatedly attempted it in the Church under the label of renewal. To pray the Apostles' Creed instead of the Nicene Creed is not a return to the zeal, the awakedness, the depth of the first Christians, but rather an artificial regress from the explicit to the implicit. Certainly the Nicene Creed contains nothing which was not contained in the faith of the apostles. But this creed is the glorious, fully articulated, explicitly developed revelation of Christ, and it directly rules out dangerous errors. Thus it is a ridiculous archaism to think that, in mentioning in the liturgy only the saints which were mentioned in the first centuries of the Church, one makes the liturgy more genuine and frees it from unessential, accidental ballast. It is rather completely in the spirit of the early church and of its devotion to the saints, that mention of later martyrs and saints be added to the liturgy. We could discuss many more examples of how the so-called return to the early Church is in no way a revival of the spirit and fervor of the early Church but rather an artificial reduction of an organic development to an earlier state in which this development was still only latent.

There is certainly also the danger of adding unessentials to the liturgy. It has for instance happened that certain prayers, which referred to temporary dangers, have remained in the liturgy by force of habit. When Pope Pius XII eliminated the prayers after Mass which Leo XIII had introduced because of a special danger, this was a case of removing something unessential from the liturgy. Or when Pius XII eliminated the Confiteor before communion at Mass, he was eliminating something unessential which had originated in the time, before Pius X, when communion was only rarely received. (St. Clare for instance lays it down in her Rule that Holy Communion should be received at least four times a year. As long as this practice of infrequent communion prevailed, the usual preparation for receiving communion outside of Mass was retained within Mass.)

But the important thing is to distinguish between unessentials which have accidentally set in, and developments which are rooted in the meaning and nature of the liturgy. This distinction becomes extremely important as soon as one wants to return not only to the spirit, the fervor and awakedness, the faithfulness and the ultimate seriousness, not only to the fight against all forms of laxity into which our human weakness so easily falls, but to return even to the external structure and forms of the early Church, its Canon Law.

But there is yet another reason which makes it dangerous to return uncritically to the forms of the early Church.

We have repeatedly said that every attempt to accommodate the teaching of the Church or even the formulation of this teaching to the spirit of the age, is based upon an utter misunderstanding of the nature of the Church. But of course it is an essential element of pastoral concern to take special notice of the dangers characteristic of an age. Thus the appeal to the early Church is very dangerous when one fails to see that we are confronted with quite different dangers today, and that in times of the most intense faith certain things may not be necessary which however in the present situation are necessary. There are for instance many aspects of the liturgy as it was celebrated in the catacombs which cannot be revived today. There was then for the Christians no danger of secularization or of a merely conventional faith. The sharp separation of them from the saeculum was effected by the persecutions. Every Mass in the catacombs put the participants in great danger and presupposed in them a living, awakened, indeed heroic faith. The very external situation of the catacombs presented a striking contrast to the spirit of the world and to the thoroughly worldly mentality of the pagans. A liturgy which under these circumstances could impress upon the souls of the faithful the real presence of Christ after the consecration, as well as the overwhelming mystery of the union of the soul with Christ in holy communion, such a liturgy would be inadequate today when a merely conventional Christianity is so widespread and when the danger is so great of being infected by the worldly, desacralized spirit of the times. Under these circumstances it is the greatest imaginable pastoral mistake to try to achieve the unity of the early Christians by having the members of the parish turn to one another and away from the glorification of God which takes place in the unbloody renewal of the sacrifice of calvary, and away from the loving union of the individual soul with Christ. The sacred unity of the Christians of the catacombs was the result of the depth and awakedness of their relation to Christ, the result of their sense for the mysterium tremendum of the holy Mass; their unity was, because of their external circumstances, so free from all secularization that we today cannot simply reinstate their liturgical forms.

Putting unity above truth: Irenicism[11]

Now that we have considered the illusion of seeing in change as such a manifestation of life (an illusion which is of course particularly dangerous when it infects persons in authority), let us turn to another widespread danger in the church which is in many respects the very opposite of this illusion.

I mean the idea that unity is more important than truth, that schism is a greater evil than heresies penetrating into the church. One often regards peace among the faithful as so important that orthodox Catholics are regarded by many prelates as uncharitable disturbers of the peace when they defend the Catholic faith against those who would give it a new interpretation and strip it of its supernatural content. To this charge we must respond as Pascal did:

> "Is it not clear that it is as much a crime to disturb the peace when truth prevails, as it is a crime to keep the peace when truth is violated. There is therefore a time when peace is justified, and a time when it is not justified. For it is written that there is a time for peace and a time for war, and it is the law of truth that distinguishes the two. But at no time is there a time for truth and a time for error, for it is written that God's truth shall abide forever. That is why Jesus Christ, who said that he will bring

peace, also said that he has come to bring war. But He does not say that He has come to bring both truth and falsehood. The truth therefore is the primary judge and the ultimate goal of things. (*Thoughts*, 949.)

It is a fundamental error to put unity above truth; moreover, true unity can only be found in the truth. Every community presupposes a domain of goods which unites the members of the community. Only when this domain possesses, not a disvalue or an illusory value, but a true value, can it form a true unity, a concordia which itself represents a value. Aristotle has seen this clearly in the chapter on friendship in his *Ethics* (cf. Books 8 and 9). The unity grounded in enmity with God is no real unity, the members of such a unity are not really bound together, any more than the criminals of a gang have any real unity among themselves. The value of unity depends upon the value of that which unites its members. As we have said, every true unity presupposes that the good which unites is really a good and not an illusory one or a pseudo-good, or a negative idol. Fr. Werenfried van Straaten is right when he writes:

"Everyone is concerned about unity, yet many prefer unity to truth and forget that true unity can be achieved only in the truth. For the prayer of Jesus, 'that all might be one,' includes that it is *in him* that all might be one; nor can this prayer of Jesus be separated from these words of his: 'I say to you, he who enters not by the door into the sheepfold,

> but climbs up another way, is a thief and a robber.
> . . . I am the door . . .' " (*Monatlicher Rundbrief*,
> December, 1969).

Every unity achieved at the expense of the truth is not
only a pseudo-unity, it is ultimately a betrayal of
God. One regards it as more important to be "brother-
ly," to "get along well" with others, not to attack
anyone, than to be faithful to God. I recall how,
after I attacked the attitude of certain German bishops
toward Nazism in my magazine, *Der Christliche Stän-
destaat,* in 1935, a Catholic professor said to me:
"How can you do such a thing! The important thing
is simply that all Catholics are united — whether
they are for or against Hitler is much less important."
That was a typical expression of the putting of
unity above truth, and of the cult of a false unity,
which prescinds from the question of truth. This is
the very opposite of the attitude of all the great fight-
ers against Arianism — of a St. Athanasius, a St.
Hilary of Poitiers, and of a St. Augustine in his fight
against Pelagianism and Donatism.[12]

The struggle against the Cross

We must now turn to the dreadful tendency to remove the cross from the life of the Christian. We need
hardly dwell on the fact that today all forms of sacrifice on a purely natural level are taboo. Our whole
system of education tries to spare children all crosses,
to fulfil their every wish; it does not call upon them
to work for their moral growth; it spares them every-

thing which is hard and laborious. But this general tendency to spoil children and to remove all sacrifice from their lives is just one of many forms of the attempt to exclude sacrifice from man's life. Now this broad tendency of our time has unfortunately infected many in the Church of Jesus Christ, of whom St. Paul says: I preach to you Jesus Christ, and Him crucified. To follow Christ without gladly taking up His cross is a self-contradiction.

Slogans such as "being fully human," "self-fulfilment" make all forms of sacrifice appear to have a crippling effect on man. One does not only try to avoid all voluntary sacrifices as well as all crosses which God imposes on us; one even claims that the sufferings which can go with the morally obligatory struggle against sins such as impurity, distort the full development of man and cause repressions.

But in reality the crosses which are necessary in the struggle against sin and which can even involve martyrdom, as in the case of St. Maria Goretti, are not only an expression of our following Christ; it is often morally obligatory to take these crosses upon ourselves.

The attempt to unite things which are mutually exclusive

But the greatest danger for Catholics and for many in the hierarchy is that they try to unite things which intrinsically exclude one another. Here I am not so much thinking of the so-called "progressivists," who no longer accept the dogmas, who deny that the resurrection of Christ historically took place, who take "science" rather than the traditional teaching of the Church as the basis of their "faith." No, I am rather thinking of those who fully hold the Catholic faith, who fully accept the Credo of Pope Paul VI, but who at the same time fall for the myth of Modern Man and believe that the Church needs a new "language" and new formulations. Or many think that they can reconcile the "theology" of Teilhard de Chardin with the Christian revelation and the teaching of the Church. Many do not even notice that in repeating the slogan, "Let us leave the Catholic ghetto and take a more positive attitude toward the world," they make a concession to the devil, who prevents them from seeing the irreconcilable and never-ending conflict between the spirit of Christ and the spirit of the world.

There are many more cases of people overlooking the incompatibility of many modern theories (which by the way are not as "new" as their defenders think, as a glance at the history of the Church shows) with the Christian faith and the teaching of the Church. Many forms of renewal which are introduced with the slogan, "Let us separate the changeable in the Church from the unchangeable," are in reality a clear withdrawal from faith in Christ and the spiritual "climate" of the Church.

It is against the background of the present intellectual and spiritual situation, of the struggle between truth and error within the Church, that we must consider the struggle for the elimination of celibacy. The less we lose sight of the dangers which threaten the Church today, which threaten her very existence, the more clearly we will see how centrally important the question of celibacy is, and what the spiritual forces are which are behind the movement to eliminate obligatory priestly celibacy.

NOTES

1. Cf. especially Ch. XII, "Evolutionism, Progressivism, and Authentic Progress," *Trojan Horse in the City of God* (Franciscan Herald Press, Chicago, 1967).

2. Cf. *Trojan Horse, op. cit.,* Ch. XVII, "The Fallacy of Homogeneous Historical Periods."

3. In his *Philosophie mediévale,* Gilson mentions various theologians who around 1250 put forward the same ideas put forward by Bultmann and the Catholic theologians influenced by him.

4. Cf. *Trojan Horse, op. cit.,* Ch. XVII, "The Fallacy of Homogeneous Historical Periods."

5. Roger Schutz, prior of the Protestant monastery of Taize, writes: "O Church of Christ, are you to become a secularized place of spiritual desolation, a dismal scene of conformity to the world, bereft of all signs of encounter with the risen Lord, salt without strength?" *Der Zoelibat,* hrsg. v. Fr. Boeckle, Gruenewaldereihe, p. 97.

6. To replace Christ by Messias is to obscure the divinity of Christ. One takes the same expression which also designates the "redeemer" which the orthodox Jews still expect and who in spite of all lack of definiteness is clearly not thought by them to be God. One pretends that such a translation is historically more exact; whereas in reality one reduces the whole difference between the faith of the orthodox

Jews and the faith of Christians to this one point: Christians regard Jesus of Nazareth as the Messias, whereas the Jews do not. But that is a distortion of the Christian faith as well as of the conviction of the apostles, as witness Peter's confession of faith (Mt. 16, 13-19) and especially the faith of all the apostles after Pentecost.

7. "It is too little to be drawn by the will; we are also drawn by delight."

8. "The love of Christ has drawn us together."

9. The famous statement of Cardinal Newman is no contradiction of what we are saying: "In a higher world it is otherwise, but here below to live is to change, and to be perfect is to have changed often." This means that we often find ourselves in circumstances where a change is objectively called for and is thus a sign of life, not that change for its own sake is a sign of life. Furthermore, Newman is here speaking of changes undertaken to preserve, for the preceding sentence is: "It (an idea in development) changes with them (its circumstances) in order to remain the same."

10. Herostratos destroyed the wonderful monument on Rhodes, called the Colossus of Rhodes, in order to become famous.

11. Von Hildebrand has an entire chapter on this subject in his book, *The Trojan Horse in the City of God* (Franciscan Herald Press, Chicago, 1967), Ch. 22. The irenicism which von Hildebrand opposes in this chapter was clearly denounced by the Council in these words: "Nothing is so foreign to the spirit of ecumenism as that false irenicism by which the purity of Catholic doctrine is defiled and its original and certain meaning is obscured." *Decree on Ecumenism*, para. 11.

12. Cardinal Newman, in his famous study of Arianism, brings out the primacy of truth over unity when he criticizes Constantine for seeing in the outbreak of the Arian heresy mainly a disturbance of the peace of the empire: "Concord is so eminently the perfection of the Christian temper . . . and it had been so wonderfully exemplified in the previous history of the Church, that it was almost unavoidable in a

heathen soldier and statesman (Constantine) to regard it as the sole precept of the Gospel. It required a far more refined moral perception, to detect and to approve the principle on which this internal peace is grounded in Scripture; to submit to the dictation of truth, as such, as a primary authority in matters of political and private conduct; to understand how . . . the social union was intended to result from an unity of opinions, the love of man to spring from the love of God, and zeal to be prior in the succession of Christian graces to benevolence." *The Arians of the Fourth Century,* pp. 243-244.

CELIBACY
and the
Crisis of Faith

Chapter I

The Distinction Between What Can Change and What Cannot Change in the Church, and Its Bearing on the Question of Celibacy

The more moderate "progressivists" often claim today that we must distinguish the changeable aspects of the church from her unchangeable aspects; that this distinction is in the interest of the Church, of her true nature, of true obedience toward her, of true faith in her; that to have made this distinction was the great achievement of the Second Vatican Council. These people say that the distinction of the changeable from the unchangeable is extremely important for the question of obligatory priestly celibacy.

Important as this distinction is, still it leads to grave errors as long as the meaning of the concepts changeable and unchangeable has not been thoroughly clarified. For as we will see, the concept changeable often encompasses very different things which should be sharply distinguished from one another.

The different meanings of the concepts changeable and unchangeable

All real essences are unchangeable. Justice for example can never become anything else, any more than the number 3 could change into something else. Although one and the same external action can now be just, now unjust, according to the situation, the essence of justice can never change. Nor can the essence of humility, charity, purity, generosity and all the other virtues ever change. And this holds for everything which possesses a real essence, as for instance the idea of truth.

Although just men can become unjust and unjust men can become just, the nature of justice cannot change; nor can any concrete act of justice ever cease to be just. All necessary and intelligible facts are unchangeable. The fact that $2 + 2 = 4$ can never change; the fact that moral values can only be possessed by persons, this fact can never change.

Let us turn to facts which are not strictly necessary such as concrete individual facts or historical events. We find that the truth of such a fact as that Caesar crossed the Rubicon in 49 B.C. is itself unchangeable. It is of course in principle possible that new historical research could show that this event did not take place, but the truth of this statement would not have thereby changed. All facts which are not immediately evident or which cannot be deduced from evident facts are never absolutely certain and there is always in principle the possibility that it will be discovered that they do not really exist. But the important thing for us to see here is that a true statement about some event is not any the less unchangeable when the event belongs to the past. The claim to truth of a statement which does not refer to necessary and intelligible facts can in principle collapse. But once the statement is true, it can not change in its truth. When a statement turns out to be false, that is no case of truth changing. The Swabian (Swabia is a region in Germany) saying, "It happened so long ago that it is hardly true any more," is humorous because so plainly false.

Now that we have seen the unchangeability of all real essences and of necessary and intelligible facts as well as of the truth of any statement, let us turn to the many changeable facts: first it is night, then day, first the sun shines, then it rains; in 1630 the Thirty Year's War was raging, but this is no longer the case today; a great cultural epoch passes away, the times change, etc. The term changeable is most precisely used where one and the same individual thing changes — for instance, in all processes of growth, whether it is the growth of a tree, of an animal, or a man in his development from child to adult.

But there is also a type of changeability which unlike the rhythm of growth in living beings is not irresistible or a law of nature. There are also many things which *can* change but do not *have to* change, as for instance the qualities of a man, above all his moral qualities. Justice, purity, humility, love and piety are indeed unchangeable in their nature and value. But as qualities of an individual man they are changeable, for they can gradually become realized in an individual man or they can disappear from him.

A man can grow in virtue — he can decline in it. He can change radically from a bad man into a good man, or from a good into a bad man; he can convert to God, or fall away from God. But he need not do any of these things. The difference between possibility and necessity is most pronounced in the moral and religious sphere, for here nothing grows or disappears without free acts of man, in other words, man is responsible for his moral and religious values and disvalues. It is quite different with intellectual values such as clarity, sharpness, and depth of mind, or with great artistic talent, for these are pure gifts. But even in the case of such nonmoral personal values, there is no strict necessity (such as we find in a law of nature) that they change. Thus the mind of an intelligent man can grow, remain the same, or deteriorate, but none of this has to happen. Rossini, for instance, produced his best work, *The Barber of Seville,* early in his artistic life, whereas only in his old age did Verdi produce his greatest works, the *Requiem, Othello,* and *Falstaff* (all composed after the age of 60). Thus even in the non-moral personal values there can be growth and decline — but this does not have to be the case.

But in our context it is above all important to distinguish between a necessary change and a merely possible change; a distinction which is particularly clearly given in the moral sphere, for here nothing happens without our freedom, or at least without our free cooperation.

The difference between what can change and what ought to change

A further difference, which is for us still more important, and which is related to the difference between possible and necessary change, is the difference between what can change and what ought to change. A man can decline in virtue, but he *ought* not. Although a man can sin, can turn away from God, can deteriorate morally, he does not have to do this, and above all, he should not do it.

We find something similar in the case of laws and institutions. The fundamental rights which God has bestowed upon man are unchangeable. But the state can deprive man of the exercise of these rights, something which every totalitarian state does. The exercise of these rights can be prohibited, but this should not happen.

That man possesses these rights is as such unchangeable and no outside force can take these from him. He can behave in such a way as to forfeit some of these rights. But even here we must emphasize that although this can happen, it need not happen, and above all, it should not happen, that is, a man should not so behave as to forfeit certain of these rights.

A tyranny often follows upon a democracy, and vice versa — but it does not have to. There is no law of nature that determines such a change, for man's freedom plays here a decisive role. And above all we have to see that the possibility of a change does not yet prove that this change ought to take place.

Those things which cannot change in the Church

All those things in the Church are clearly unchangeable which in their value and validity are independent from all development in time and from a given historical and cultural situation. Thus all dogmas are clearly unchangeable. All truths of the deposit of the Catholic faith are unchangeable. Thus all contradictions among the dogmas are impossible. This belongs to the nature of the infallibility of the Church.

The dogmas are intrinsically unchangeable in their meaning just as every absolute truth is unchangeable. First of all, the dogmas cannot cease to be valid; second, they cannot change; finally, their validity is in no way relative to any historical development. The most that even an atheist can meaningfully say of the dogmas is that they are not true — that the facts to which they refer do not really exist. But not

even an atheist can say that their validity is changeable or can pass away or is limited to a certain period
of time. They are either true or false. If they are true,
they are eternal, unchangeable, and in their validity
independent of the rhythm of time — otherwise they
must be false, that is, that to which they refer never
was the case. But they can never be changeable,
temporary, or limited in their validity to a certain
period of time. In the same way the nature of the
holiness, which all Christians in following Christ must
strive for, is unchangeable. This holiness is one and
the same for all times, indeed it is the same for time
and eternity.

The question for us is: what belongs to the nature
of the Catholic Church, what belongs to her in such
a way that she would lose her identity without it;
and what is only factually present in her without
belonging to her nature?

The divine institution of the Church, her infallible
magisterium which is protected by the Holy Ghost,
her character as mystical body of Christ, her authoritative and hierarchical structure — all this belongs
to the nature of the Church. The institution of the
Church by Christ, the birth of the Church at Pentecost, and the apostolic succession also belong to the
nature of the Church — whoever denies these necessarily denies that which the Church claims to be, for
without these facts the church of Christ would lose
her identity.

No characteristic belonging to the nature of a thing can be eliminated without changing the nature of that thing.[1]

Similarly the power of consecration presupposes the sacrament of Holy Orders. The relation between this sacrament and the power of consecration at the holy Mass is an unchangeable element of the Church. God could indeed have established it otherwise — but the decree of a pope giving every layman the power of consecration would clearly be invalid, it would exceed the competence of the Church, because it would contradict the relation between power of consecration and Holy Orders which has been dogmatically established.

Among the changeable elements of the Church some should be changed, others should not

All decrees, all Canon Law are in principle changeable, as are all enactments which appeal to obedience (except when their content logically follows from the deposit of the Catholic faith).

In this sense obligatory priestly celibacy in the Western Church clearly does not belong to the unchangeable elements of the Church but rather to the changeable.[2]

As long as we only observe that something in the Church is changeable because it does not belong to her nature, we have not yet said anything about the value of this changeable thing. However much superior the unchangeable elements of the Church are to the changeable in their importance and rank, still the changeability of some ordinance or arrangement tells us nothing about its value and thus nothing as to whether it should be eliminated or not. Here begins the dangerous equivocation with the term changeable. One often uses it in a completely different sense: in the sense that certain institutions, laws, etc. are good and useful in a certain situation, in a certain historical period, but that they lose their value and meaning when the circumstances change. Thus, for instance, the limitation of certain freedoms is necessary in time of war, and many laws which are good and useful during the war, lose their value and even become unjustified as soon as the war is over. Such laws are thus typically changeable and are opposed to the unchangeable moral laws.

The fact that a thing is relative to a certain situation and historical period must be sharply distinguished from the fact that a thing emerged at a certain point in history. *The fact that something has not always existed and was introduced at a certain point in history, proves neither that it is relative in its value to this point in history, nor that its elimination would be an improvement.*

When one distinguishes changeable things in the Church from unchangeable, the question of which of the changeable things ought to be changed remains completely unanswered. And if one means by the concept changeable that changeable things are relative to a certain historical period and certain circumstances, then by no means is everything which has emerged in time changeable.

The crass ambiguity of the concept changeable: In principle changeable, and out of date

One often tacitly includes in the concept changeable the idea that the importance, value, indeed justification of the changeable things in the Church are relative to a certain time. It is quite usual to hear one argue for a change in the rules of some religious order in this way: "That was fine for the people of 1550, but let us not forget that we are now living in 1970." One takes it for granted that every rule, every arrangement, the whole of Canon Law must be changed because the times have changed — one fails to distinguish three completely different questions: 1) Is something in principle changeable? 2) Is a changeable thing good and valuable? 3) Is it good and valuable only for a certain historical period, does its justification depend on certain historical circumstances?

In speaking of the changeable things in the Church, many people actually mean that long-standing practices are old-fashioned and out of date. A great confusion is at the bottom of this mindless talk — and sometimes even a sophistical dishonesty. One sneaks into the concept of changeability the quite different concept of the relativity of some value to certain historical circumstances. We could put it this way: one pretends that being old-fashioned, being out of date necessarily belongs to the concept of changeable. The first step is to identify the changeable in the Church with that which depends on time and history — to identify the fact that something can in principle change, with the fact that it can in its meaning and value be made obsolete with the passage of history. The second step is then to argue from the changeability of a thing to the fact that it has become obsolete and should be eliminated or replaced by something new. One says, it might have had a value in earlier times but now, having become obsolete, it has lost its value, and *should* be eliminated.

Obligatory priestly celibacy is indeed in principle changeable, but by no means therefore outdated

Since obligatory celibacy belongs to the changeable things in the Church, those who want to give a reason for abolishing it find it convenient to include the idea of obsolescence in that of changeability.[3] But it has to be forcefully emphasized that this jump from changeable to obsolete is completely illegitimate. That which is changeable in the sense discussed above can possess a great permanent value and does not at all have to become obsolete.

No one doubts that obligatory priestly celibacy does not belong to the unchangeable elements of the Church such as the dogmas, the moral teaching of the Church, and the sacraments.

But the changeability of celibacy, which is opposed

to the unchangeability of these things, does not, as we see, involve any relativizing of the value of celibacy.

As long as this equivocation prevails, a serious discussion about obligatory celibacy is impossible, and the important distinction between changeable and unchangeable is reduced to an empty slogan.

For the separation of the changeable from the unchangeable intends to separate those things in the Church which should always remain the same, from those things which are relative to a certain time, are without enduring value, and should be, when no longer useful, eliminated. An example of such a changeable thing would be the Papal State, which undoubtedly had a great significance in the Middle Ages and served an important purpose but which eventually could be eliminated without forfeiting something of high value. Here then is something which in its value really was relative to a certain time.

The distinction of changeable from unchangeable in this sense is very important for giving the right response to the hierarchy of values.[4] A true faith requires that we do justice to the hierarchy of values. Just as our faith should clearly distinguish the dogmas from a mere communis opinio (generally held opinion), so we should also clearly distinguish the laws of God as well as all laws deriving from the moral teaching of the Church from all merely positive laws of the Church. Many Catholics and even some religious and priests are often not clear on this point.[5]

Whether obligatory priestly celibacy should be abolished or retained in the Western Church depends exclusively on whether it has a high value and a deep meaning which is no way relative to a particular historical period or whether it no longer has any value today and should be abolished in light of new circumstances. We repeat: to observe that celibacy does not belong to the very nature of the priesthood (a fact which no one denies) is not to prove that obligatory celibacy should be abolished. It is an altogether sufficient reason for retaining celibacy if it is more adequate to the meaning and nature of the priesthood, even though it does not belong intrinsically to the nature of the priesthood. Only if it were more adequate for a priest to marry than to remain unmarried propter regnum coelorum (for the sake of the kingdom of heaven) would the abolition of obligatory celibacy be desirable. Indeed, even if marrying and remaining unmarried were equally adequate to the priesthood, that is, even if both accorded equally well with the meaning and nature of the priesthood, there would be no reason to abolish obligatory celibacy as long as celibacy had a high value on other grounds.

In the following we will see that there is a deeply meaningful relation between celibacy and the meaning and nature of the priesthood, that celibacy, while not intrinsically belonging to the priesthood, is still far more adequate to it. We will see the high value of priestly celibacy. We will see that obligatory celibacy is not only not outdated today, but that it takes on a special, increased importance precisely at the present time and especially in the present crisis in the Church.[6]

In the next chapter we will try to reflect on the nature, the greatness, and beauty of the office of the priest. Then, in the third chapter, which will be on the nature of celibacy, we will consider first the great gift which marriage is, then the great sacrifice of giving it up, and finally the glory of renouncing it for the sake of the kingdom of heaven.

This is the necessary background for investigating the affinity between the priesthood and celibacy. Only against this background can we understand whether celibacy is more adequate to the priesthood, and to what extent.

NOTES

1. We must now make a further important distinction. There are indispensable conditions which are grounded in the nature of a thing or are intrinsically and necessarily connected with it. Thus the act of promising creates an obligation towards the person to whom one makes the promise, in other words, the promise gives this person a right to that which is promised. We have to distinguish now such intrinsic features of the promise from those which can be added by positive law. In some countries only written promises are legally valid; in these countries this condition (that a promise must be written) must be fulfilled before an obligation can be created, but this condition is not intrinsically and necessarily connected with the obligation deriving from a promise. The relation between promise and

obligation obtains *before* all positive law and independently of it. But legislative authority has by its nature the special power of making the realization of certain things depend upon conditions which do not belong to the nature of those things. But the legislative authority cannot validly ignore the intrinsic and necessary presuppositions and relations of these things, even less can it contradict them by a positive law. It can only add conditions under which these things can be realized — under which, in our example, an obligation can be effectively established by a promise. A. Reinach has clearly shown all this in his masterpiece, *Das Apriori im Buergerlichen Recht* (Munich, 1953).

The important thing for us to see here is that intrinsic conditions are unchangeable, whereas the conditions added by legislative authority — as for instance all positive laws — are in principle changeable. Let us consider another example of the difference between intrinsically constitutive and positively (we use this word in the sense of positive law) constitutive. Marriage necessarily and intrinsically presupposes the consensus of the two; without this consensus a marriage could never, under any circumstance, come into existence. The relation between consensus and marriage is an intrinsic, necessary, unchangeable relation. But it does not belong to the nature of marriage that, as distinguished from earlier times in the church, the consensus of a valid marriage must be given, not before just any witness, but before a priest in a Catholic church, and that the marriage must be blessed by him; these are rather further conditions laid down by the legislative authority of the Church, that is, they belong to the positive laws of the Church and are in principle changeable.

2. Cf. the encyclical of Pope Paul "On Priestly Celibacy," para. 17: "Virginity undoubtedly, as the Second Vatican Council declared, 'is not, indeed, demanded by the very nature of the priesthood, as is evident from the practice of the primitive Church and from the tradition of the Eastern Churches' " (Decr. Presbyterorum Ordinis, n. 16).

3. Some want to eliminate obligatory priestly celibacy,

not only on the grounds that it is outdated, but also on the grounds that it is an "adiaphoron" (an indifferent matter), as if it were an unimportant, more or less bureaucratic matter.

Such persons compare obligatory celibacy with the question with which the apostles were confronted, whether all the Jewish legal prescriptions should be binding on non-Jewish Christians, whether they should be a presupposition for the receiving of pagans into the Church of Christ. And then one appeals to the view of St. Paul, which eventually prevailed. But it is obvious that this comparison limps. In the case of obligatory celibacy we are dealing with something which was expressly introduced as being more adequate to the meaning and mission of the priest and as possessing (as we will see later) a great enduring value, whereas in the case of the Jewish prescriptions we are dealing with something having no intrinsic connection with the Christian faith and with membership in the Christian Church. The elimination of these prescriptions, which from the point of view of the Christian revelation were no longer of value, was a normal step in the process of the emergence of the Church.

Furthermore, in speaking of entrance into the Church, we are speaking of a call addressed to every man. According to the words of Christ, "Go and teach all nations, . . . " every man is obliged to follow this call. To require celibacy of priests cannot be compared with making membership in the Church dependent on something (the Jewish prescriptions) which was only historically connected with the Christian revelation but which was rendered obsolete by it. For the call to the priesthood is not directed to every man and is not a condition for following Christ and belonging to his mystical body. Obligatory celibacy is more adequate to the meaning and nature of the priesthood and can thus clearly not be compared with requiring the Jewish prescriptions of the gentile Christians.

4. On this subject cf. the author's *Liturgy and Personality* (Baltimore, Helicon Press, 1960), especially the passage beginning: "However, the decisive feature of true personality is not only the fundamental response-to-value attitude. . . .

True personality also demands a clear understanding of the *hierarchy of values,* the preponderance to be given to the greater value, and the renunciation, for its sake, of what is less important. In this inner conformity to the objective order of values lies the secret of true personality" (p. 59).

5. Thus a religious once said to me in America: why should we not grant that moral laws can change, when eating meat on Friday was a grave sin before the Council but is now allowed. This confusion is very revealing: he confused merely positive laws of the Church which can in principle be abolished, with moral laws which are rooted in the unchangeability of moral values and ultimately in the nature of God himself.

6. It is of course a danger for many men to regard that to which they are accustomed as absolute and unchangeable. Just as there are many men who cannot distinguish the essential from the unessential, so there are many men who, because accustomed to something, having never experienced it otherwise, cannot distinguish it from that which is intrinsically unchangeable. Indeed, such men no longer ask whether it has a value or not, they just treat it as if it should never be abolished or changed — in other words, they treat it as if it had a high value. This is certainly the source of many grave errors. But, on the other hand, there are certainly also many men who let themselves be so influenced by changes in the times that they regard everything new and modern as an improvement; they do not understand the high value of many things which should not be changed. They think rather that anyone who fights for the preservation of something is only a slave of custom. These are the men who swim with the tide of the times and who are carried away by the dynamism of those ideas which are "in the air." But there are also many men who are intoxicated by "movement" as such ("movement is everything, the goal is only secondary" — this sentiment was typical of many youth movements before the second World War), to whom every change appears as a triumph over ossification, the influx of fresh air.

Chapter II
The Office of the Priest

In order truly to understand sublime natural goods we must achieve an attitude of reverence, wondering, marveling, which Plato and Aristotle regard as necessary for all true philosophy. But this is much more the case, indeed it is the case in a completely new way when we turn to the divine revelation in and through Christ, to the sacraments, and to the holy Church herself. We must prepare ourselves for our reflections on the priesthood by recollecting ourselves and being filled with deep reverence for the unspeakable gift of God which the priesthood is. We of course do not intend to offer a theological treatise on the priesthood but rather a brief meditation on its nature and dignity.

The power of consecration and the administration of the sacraments

At the center of the office of the priest is his power to consecrate. St. Francis of Assisi expressed his reverence for all priests in these words: "If I were at the same time to meet a priest and St. Lawrence, I would

21

first kiss the hand of the priest and say: 'Forgive me, St. Lawrence, but the hands of the priest touch the body of our Lord each day!' " The unique dignity which is bestowed on the office of the priest because he has received in Holy Orders the power to consecrate, attaches to his *office* as priest and not to his person. Even if he were a great sinner, he would not lose this power. Whether a saint or a sinner, he equally possesses the power of consecration — indeed, even if he falls away from the Church he does not lose this power.[1]

In considering this we are confronted with the sublime grandeur of the office of the priest — and with the great difference between a layman and a priest. And let us consider further that it is the priest who administers the sacraments — that he normally possesses the unique privilege of directing the flow of grace into souls, of presenting the faithful with this unspeakable gift of God. But this great mission is linked with the office of the priest in a different way, according to the type of sacrament. Only a priest can absolve sins in the sacrament of penance. In order to be able to absolve he needs, except in extraordinary situations, such as *in articulo mortis* (at the point of death), the authorization of the local bishop. Thus he cannot simply begin hearing confessions in a diocese other than his own, he must first receive permission from the vicar general of this other diocese. Only in certain emergencies can he hear confession without this permission.

But on the other hand only a priest and never a layman can hear confession and validly absolve. But a layman can validly baptize under urgent circumstances when a priest cannot be reached; a layman can also give communion in extraordinary cases, as for instance St. Tarcisius did and as was sometimes done in the Nazi concentration camps or as is done today in the mission countries.

The grandeur of the office of the priest stands out again when we consider that by his office he shares in the unspeakable supernatural power which Christ bestowed on the apostles with these words: "Whatever you will bind on earth, will be bound in heaven . . . "

We must recall how the Pharisees were scandalized when Jesus forgave the cripple his sins, in order to grasp in its full breadth the supernatural character of absolution (which is actually reserved for God alone). We cannot sufficiently marvel at what an unimagineable gift it is that Christ conferred this power, which he as God-man had, upon the apostles (and through them upon their followers), and that every priest shares in this power. How must every priest tremble when he realizes how he is joined to Christ by his office and his faculties of absolving the faithful of their sins in the name of Christ, when he realizes that in giving absolution Christ touches the soul of the sinner in a unique way, frees him from his guilt, and restores him to the state of grace.

The sublime grandeur of the office of the priest is also shown in the fact that he is entrusted with administering the other sacraments (except in special emergencies).

It is an unimagineable gift and a marvel that there are men who live only to glorify God through the sacrifice of the Mass, to direct the flow of grace into the souls of the faithful, and who totally belong to the Church. Now the priest has, in addition to these duties, the further duty of proclaiming the word of God.

Proclaiming the word of God in the "world"

It is a great thing to preach the word of God to the faithful in the name of the holy Church; in the midst of the world — where the noise of the saeculum is today greater than ever because of the mass media, and where souls are ensnared in the net of the prince of this world — it is the holy Church and in her name the priest who "in season, out of season" proclaims the great call of God: "Jerusalem convertere ad Dominum Deum tuum" ("Jerusalem, convert to the Lord your God"). We must reflect on the struggle between Christ and the spirit of the "world" which will last until the end of time, if we are to grasp this aspect of the greatness of the office of the priest. We cannot be sufficiently grateful for the gift of having men whose calling in life is to oppose the tide of the times in the world, to preach to the faithful the divine revelation of Christ which is contained in the deposit of the Catholic faith of the holy Church, who give the faithful this sacred spiritual nourishment. This also shows us the dignity of the office of the priest. It is a being-in-the-world yet without being of the world which is objectively contained in the office of the priest.

Establishing the Kingdom of God, and saving souls

Every priest is also called to be a missionary, that is, it belongs to his office as organ of the Church and as soldier of God equipped with the unique authority *deriving from his office,* to establish the kingdom of God in the souls of men — to do this first of all in the souls of the faithful committed to him, and then, wherever the opportunity presents itself, to win for Christ and lead into his Church those souls who have not yet found him or do not yet belong to his holy Church.

His mission is the kingdom of God and the salvation of souls. He dedicates his life to this mission. He is of course also called to help the poor of his parish, to comfort the suffering, to encourage those who are humiliated and suffering injustice. But the meaning of the priesthood above all — in what concerns his flock if he is a parish priest, or in what concerns the men with whom he deals if he is for instance a teacher — is to be concerned for the sanctification of souls and their eternal salvation. The priest is not a welfare official. The motto for every Christian: "Seek first the kingdom of God and his justice," is the very soul of the office of the priest. The raison d'etre of the Church is to establish the kingdom of Christ in the souls of the faithful, to give glory to God through their sanctification, and to work for their eternal salvation. This means that the priest fights against evil, against the prince of this world, against all attempts to spread errors and to lead the souls of men away from God by false teachings — and this fight includes above all the clear condemnation of all heresies. Now it is also the raison d'etre of the office of the priest to be an organ of the holy Church and to share in her office. It is also the meaning and nature of *his* office to strive to establish the kingdom of God in the souls of men, to pour into their souls the flow of grace in the sacraments, to proclaim the word of God, to protect them from the onslaught of false teachings.[2]

Thus our Holy Father says: "Like Christ himself, his minister is wholly and solely intent on the things of God and the Church, and he imitates the great high Priest who stands in the presence of God ever living to intercede for us . . . "[3] "The priest with grace and peace in his heart will face with generosity the manifold tasks of his life and ministry. If he performs these with faith and zeal he will find in

them new occasions to show that he belongs entirely
to Christ and his Mystical Body, for his own sanctification and the sanctification of others."[4]

NOTES

1. This power becomes ineffective only when the priest
in saying the words of consecration does not have the *intention* of the Church; when for instance he wants to consecrate with a blasphemous intention, or when he considers
his "consecration" as only symbolic.

2. What Cardinal Newman says of the Church applies
to the priest: "The Church aims, not at making a show,
but at doing a work. She regards this world, and all that is
in it, as a mere shadow, as dust and ashes, compared with
the value of one single soul. She holds that, unless she can,
in her own way, do good to souls, it is no use her doing
anything; she holds that it were better for sun and moon to
drop from heaven, for the earth to fail, and for all the
many millions who are upon it to die of starvation in ex-
tremest agony, so far as temporal affliction goes, than that
one soul, I will not say, should be lost, but should commit
one single venial sin, should tell one wilful untruth, though
it harmed no one, or steal one poor farthing without excuse.
She considers the action of this world and the action of the
soul simply incommensurate, viewed in their respective
spheres; she would rather save the soul of one single wild
bandit of Calabria, or whining beggar of Palermo, than
draw a hundred lines of railroad through the length and
breadth of Italy, or carry out a sanitary reform, in its fullest
details, in every city of Sicily, except so far as these great
national works tended to some spiritual good beyond them."
Difficulties of Anglicans, vol. 1 (Longmans, Green, and
Co., London, 1897), pp. 239-240.

3. On Priestly Celibacy, para. 28.

4. *Ibid.,* para. 76.

Chapter III
The Nature of Celibacy

Many see in celibacy primarily a renunciation of sexual satisfaction. The argument is: the sexual instinct is after all something which God has implanted in the nature of man, and the desire to satisfy this instinct is thoroughly legitimate. One calls it Manichean to see this instinct as something evil and taboo. One thinks that in calling upon a man to give up fulfilling this side of his nature, we are crippling him; then one introduces all the Freudian arguments, one points for instance to the complexes which are supposed to result unavoidably from celibacy, etc. But in our context it is important to see that those who argue like this do not see the sacrifice of celibacy to lie in renouncing the communion of love in marriage, but rather in renouncing legitimate sexual satisfaction. And unfortunately we encounter this view not only among the enemies of obligatory celibacy but sometimes even among its defenders. This misunderstanding of the meaning and value of marriage as well as of the purpose and mystery of the sensual

29

sphere in man, is a disastrous error and distorts the whole problem of priestly celibacy.

On the nature of marriage

And so we have to reflect first of all on the nature of marriage and its great dignity — as well as the fact that it is such a great gift that it can be the source of man's greatest earthly happiness; we say "can," for we should not forget how rare it is for a marriage to be in every respect truly happy. But this is true of all great earthly goods which are sources of deep happiness, such as deep and significant professional work, children, etc.

But here in our consideration of the renunciation of so great a good as marriage, we want to focus on the nature of marriage and not on the possibility of this nature being imperfectly realized.

We want to achieve an awareness of what a source of happiness marriage can be according to its true nature.

Many passages of Holy Scripture refer to the great dignity of marriage and regard it so highly as to choose it "as an image of the relationship between God and the soul. It is an image in the sense that an imperfect picture represents a perfect model, on the Old Testament prefigures the New. Indeed, Jesus is called the *spouse* of the soul, and the Canticle of Canticles presents the union of Christ with the soul as a bridal union. Why does Holy Scripture choose precisely marriage as a comparison? Because marriage is the closest and most intimate of all earthly unions; because in it more than in any other, one person gives himself to another without reserve; the other as a whole is the object of love as in no other human relationship; mutual love itself is in a unique way the theme of this relationship."[1]

"The charm exercised by human love," says Pope Pius XII speaking of spousal love, "has been for centuries the inspiring theme of admirable works of genius, in literature, in music, in the visual arts; a theme always old and always new, upon which the ages have embroidered, without ever exhausting it, the most elevated and poetic variations."[2]

And this love finds its fulfilment in marriage. The true meaning of the physical union in marriage and of the sensual sphere in man is, apart from procreation, the union desired by spousal love. It is again Pope Pius XII who has magnificently expressed this: "The conjugal act, in its natural structure, is a personal action, a simultaneous and immediate cooperation of husband and wife, which, owing to the very nature of the agents and the propriety of the act, is the expression of the mutual self-donation, which, according to the words of Scripture, effects the union 'in one flesh.' "[3]

And the union which spousal love desires is achieved not only in this deepest self-donation, but also in all forms of affection, in the one life which both lead together, in the constant presence of the beloved.

But a completely new and much deeper union of love in marriage is present when the two encounter one another in Christ. Pius XII magnificently expressed this too: "But what new and unutterable beauty is added to this love of two human hearts, when its song is harmonized with the hymn of two souls vibrating with supernatural life! Here, too, there is an exchange of gifts; and then, through bodily tenderness and its healthy joys, through natural affection and its impulses, through a spiritual union and its delights, the two beings who love each other identify themselves in all that is most intimate in them, from the unshaken depths of their beliefs to the highest summit of their hopes."[4] When we consider the happiness which spousal love bestows when husband and wife look lovingly at one another, when the love of each for the other is requited by the other, then we can understand what a source of happiness, what a gift marriage is in man's life.

And then there is the happiness which the children bring, the fruit of the union of love — what an unimaginable gift, to be able to share in the coming into being of a new human being. As it is expressed in the old Fulda ritual: "O Lord God, thou hast created man pure and without blemish and hast ordained that in the propagation of the human race one generation should proceed from the other through the mystery of sweet love."

Celibacy involves then the renunciation of a great good, the unique communion of love in marriage, the deepest source of natural happiness on earth.

Loneliness does not necessarily result from being unmarried

Some people emphasize that remaining unmarried not only involves renouncing the legitimate development of man's sensual side in marriage, but also involves loneliness. But marriage is incomparably more than, indeed is something radically different from, the mere antithesis to loneliness. The loneliness of a person can be eliminated by living with persons dear to him, with a mother, a sister, or with friends. We have to distinguish here two forms of loneliness, an external and an inward, human loneliness. External loneliness comes from living alone, from being alone in daily life. A person is lonely in this sense when his daily life is not a natural being together with others whom he does not dislike. This loneliness is overcome when a priest lives in a parish with other priests who are his friends or with whom he at least gets along, or when his mother or a sister or a devout and dedicated housekeeper keeps house for him. The inward, human loneliness is eliminated when someone has a relation of deep mutual understanding with one or several persons, and loves them and is loved by them; whether these persons are the parents of the priest, or brothers or sisters, or friends is unimportant. The important thing is that there are persons whom one loves deeply, with whom one is bound by a deep mutual understanding, with whom one can be together from time to time. The inward, human loneliness is by no means necessarily involved in celibacy.

A priest therefore does not have to be at all lonely in this sense simply because he lives in celibacy; how many priests have not been at all lonely in this sense! What a great role his mother Margareta played in Don Bosco's life! What a great role friendships played in the life of St. Augustine, of St. Jerome, of Cardinal Newman! Whether one is humanly lonely does not depend on whether one is a priest or a layman, it rather depends on one's character and above all on whether God grants the great gift of finding persons whom one loves deeply (of course not with spousal love) and with whom a bond of deep mutual understanding is established. A layman can just as well become humanly lonely as a priest.[5] Even in marriage one can be lonely.

But marriage is incomparably more than the absence of external and inward, human loneliness. First, marital love is a unique source of happiness in itself, a fact which has so often been eloquently expressed in music and poetry. Second, this mutual love strives for a union which cannot be compared with any other human union — the union of marriage. Here the external living together mentioned above takes on a quite different character: here there is an identification of lives. Man and wife do not just live together, they are not just naturally together in all the situations of life — life has become for them in principle one life, a fact beautifully expressed in their sharing the same name. They solemnly agree to identify their personal lives. And in addition to all this the mutual self-donation in the marital act establishes a unique unity of man and wife. This is incomparably greater and more important, it bestows incomparably more happiness, than the satisfaction of the sexual instinct and the elimination of loneliness.

Priestly celibacy and the sacrifice of remaining unmarried

It was certainly a great mistake when marriage was portrayed to seminarians in as unattractive a light as possible. On the contrary the greatness of this sacrifice must be emphasized, as well as the special charisma which is required to renounce marriage for the sake of Christ. But as we will see, this willingness to sacrifice for the sake of Christ is linked with the priesthood in a deeply meaningful way. When we grasp the greatness and the sacredness of the office of the priest — speaking in the name of the Church, totally belonging to the Church, administering the sacraments, and above all the power to consecrate — we understand that the sacrifice which the priest makes in accepting celibacy is small in comparison with the gift which he receives in being able to be a priest of the holy Church.

Celibate priests are not just bachelors

We have to see the abyss which separates a mere
bachelor from the celibate priest. There are certainly
many distinctions to be made with regard to bachelors.
There is a type of man who remains a bachelor out
of egoism, out of fear of the self-donation to another
person, of the consideration for him, the interest in
him, which marriage involves. There are bachelors
who are incapable of falling in love, whose tempera-
ment keeps them from ever marrying. Then there are
men who do not marry because they have never
found the person whom they could really love; and
finally there are men who have loved someone who
either did not love them in return or was already
married. However different these various bachelor
types are, still priestly celibacy represents something
utterly new over against all forms of simply remaining
unmarried. Priestly celibacy is a renunciation of marriage for the sake of the kingdom of heaven, it is a
unique form of self-donation to Christ. It is not a
way of being resigned to remaining unmarried, even
less is it a typical bachelor-attitude, an inability to
give oneself to another, a shrinking back from the
considerateness for the other which goes with loving
him; it is rather a glorious way of remaining unmarried which grows out of total self-donation to
Christ[6] and the desire to be free for the duties which
go with the priesthood. When someone feels himself
called to the priesthood, he must also feel the call to

belong totally to the Church and to the priesthood as an organ of the Church.

The great and noble sacrifice contained in celibacy is, as we saw, the renunciation of marriage, of the most intimate human communion of love, of this central source of man's natural happiness, and the renunciation of the great gift of having children. As soon as one sees marriage only as a legitimate occasion for satisfying the sexual instinct, one has misunderstood the meaning and value of marriage, and in misunderstanding this, one also misunderstands the real sacrifice which is offered to God in accepting celibacy for the sake of the kingdom of heaven.

But of course many persons are subject to isolated sexual temptations. It is the duty of every man and especially of every Christian not to give in to these temptations, to overcome them consciously and deliberately. Even a married person may have to continue to struggle in this respect: not with regard to satisfying the sexual instinct but rather with regard to overemphasizing the purely sensual aspect of the marital act. Mutual self-donation and the fulfilment of the union with the beloved which spousal love desires, should have absolute primacy; but this can be destroyed when sexual satisfaction is overemphasized. I have discussed this at length in my book, *In Defense of Purity*. This concerns purity in marriage. But as long as someone is not married he is morally obliged to fight against isolated sexual desires (which are a result of original sin). Even a priest can still be engaged in this struggle — but this is not a consequence of his celibacy. This is a struggle for every man who is unmarried, for whatever reason. Of course the unmarried man has not renounced for good the satisfaction of sexual desire; he could yet marry, and then this satisfaction is allowed to him. In renouncing marriage for good, one has no longer even the possibility of having this satisfaction without sin. But on the other hand there is in the virginity dedicated to God a tremendous help for overcoming all these temptations.

The nature of celibacy and how it can be misunderstood

The total self-donation to God, dwelling in his holy temple, sealing off the sensual sphere, dying to oneself for Christ, all this does not emasculate or neutralize the celibate; it is rather a triumphant anticipation of eternity "where there is neither marrying nor giving in marriage."[7] But when one completely turns away from this sphere — which in no way implies a negative attitude toward it — isolated sexual desires are reduced.

The important thing is to grasp the radical difference between a repression and the conscious, deliberate sealing off of this sphere for Christ's sake. In the case of a repression one forces oneself to look away from this sphere, one does not admit its reality, or one tries to see it in a negative light so as to make the sacrifice easier; one tries to make this sphere seem repulsive. I am not thereby saying that it does not happen that a priest really does repress this sphere instead of sealing it off in the right way for Christ's sake. But the fact that something beautiful and sublime can be replaced by something negative is a tragic possibility of our fallen nature which can occur in all areas and in every situation. Cannot a good deed be stripped of its moral value when the man who does it proudly admires his moral excellence? Does it not often happen that a man and a woman marry, not because they deeply love one another but because they want to satisfy legitimately a vehement sensuality? Or does it not often happen that someone marries because he is afraid of the social image of an unfulfilled life, of one who was unable to find a partner for marriage? The possibility that an attitude can be distorted is neither an objection against the value of the right attitude nor an objection against the essential and radical difference between the right attitude and its distortion. The possibility of slipping from a noble, good attitude into a quite different negative attitude does not eliminate the radical qualitative difference between the two.[8]

No — the conscious sealing off of the sexual sphere, the reverent self-donation to Christ in thus dying to oneself, is separated by an abyss from sexual repression; nor are these things any the less different simply because a man can repress the sexual sphere instead of sealing it off in the right way, or can fall from the one attitude into the other, especially in the course of time. This can happen, but it does not have to happen.

We must go into the depths if we are going adequately to grasp the reality of great goods and also of terrible evils, if we are going to see as they really are things possessing a value or disvalue. On the one hand we must, as already mentioned, actualize a special kind of marveling, on the other hand we must be completely attentive to the voice of being, we must open ourselves to reality and not allow any "theories" to get between reality and our receptive spiritual powers. We have to be truly receptive, and we have to be the more receptive, the higher the value to which we address ourselves.

But also something else is required. If we are to grasp the valid, authentic nature of a good, we have to reflect on the highest realization of this good and not on cases where it is present in a mediocre, watered-down way or even in a distorted way. Even the question of how often the true nature of some good is fully realized (for instance, how often happy marriages occur) is not decisive for the nature of that good.[9]

But when we are dealing with religious goods, indeed with everything belonging to the relation between God and man, and especially with sacred things, then an even greater reverence and a special depth is required in order to see these things in their true light. What St. Anselm says in his *Proslogion* about the knowledge of God applies in an analogous way to the entire domain of religion: we can only hope to understand something if we have first of all prayed. It is in this spirit that we must approach the virginity consecrated to God if we are going to understand its meaning and value, to understand it in its greatness and beauty.

Priestly celibacy is understandable only on the basis of faith

We have to realize also that abstinence for the sake of the kingdom of heaven, the sealing off of the sensual sphere, renouncing the greatest source of human happiness — the communion of love in marriage — is not only an expression of ultimate love for Christ but also a unique manifestation of faith in him. If we ask how many things we do and how many sacrifices we make in life which have their meaning only in the light of faith, which are only meaningful if the Christian revelation is true, we find that there are relatively few such things. Most actions have a meaning independent of faith, even when their meaning and value receive a completely new importance and a new light through faith. But all professional work, all scientific research, all philosophical insight, all artistic creation, all communion with beloved persons, marriage, family, friendship, all have a meaning and value even apart from faith.

Of course the terrible tragedy of an unredeemed world, where we "sit in the shadow of death," where there is no God, no redemption through Christ, no eternal life, this tragedy pervades all the goods of man's life, all his actions, indeed his whole existence. But that does not prevent all the above-mentioned activities or acts of man from being performed on motives which do not presuppose faith (nor does it prevent many sacrifices from being made without faith). One cannot say even of the believing man who does everything in the name of Christ and offers everything up to God, that he would do none of this if he had no faith.

But praying, participating in the sacrifice of the Mass, the sacraments, these presuppose faith in such a way that it is their only meaningful motive.

Of course all merely ascetical sacrifices such as fasting when it is done from purely religious motives (in obligatory fasting the motive is also obedience to the Church) are done only for the sake of Christ. But the type and greatness of the sacrifice in fasting cannot be compared with that which a man gives up in the vow of virginity or abstinence. When we reflect on the greatness of the gift of marriage, on its sublime value, on the depth of the happiness which it can bestow, then it becomes clear that celibacy is a unique manifestation of faith, that it is one of the few things which can be motivated only by faith and by love of Christ. It is the faith that this earthly existence is only a status viae and that the real, truly valid fulfilment lies in eternity, the status termini.

In this vow a man also transfers into eternity the yearning for happiness and the expectation of happiness which is so deeply rooted in man. This act is the expression of triumph over the world — which is our faith. Here faith becomes unconditional: a man does not want to enjoy life and hope for eternity, but rather choses a state of life in which he burns[10] his bridges behind him and lives only from faith.

Dangers threatening the celibacy of individual priests

Of course I am speaking here only of the greatness and value of this act as such. It is clear that not all the various temptations to pride and concupiscence are eliminated by taking this vow. Each of us has to struggle against the dangers of our fallen nature right up to our last breath — even though this struggle varies greatly from individual to individual, and is, in the case of the saint, of a different kind. The admonition of St. Peter, "Brethren, be sober, be watchful," will always apply to us as long as we are in statu viae.[11]

It can easily happen that the holy emptiness resulting from celibacy and the renunciation of marriage for the sake of the kingdom of heaven, though it should be filled by Christ and by working for the kingdom of God in the souls of men, will in fact be filled by other things, such as scientific research,

desire for fame, taking pleasure in ruling others —
the type of substitute depends on the particular type
of activity of the priest or religious. It belongs to the
meaning of the act in which a man vows celibacy,
that he is conscious of these dangers and specially
struggles against them lest other earthly sources of
happiness surreptitiously substitute for the renunciation of marriage and play a role which contradicts the
heroic self-donation of celibacy, indeed, which threat-
ens to undermine the real meaning of celibacy.

But as we saw not even the struggle against the
flesh is at an end when the vow of celibacy is taken.
But this does not diminish the greatness, the sublimity,
and the value of this vow, all of which are realized
when the celibate fully recognizes the link with
Christ contained in celibacy and when he renews in
himself each day the full spirit of celibacy.

The priesthood and the vocation to celibacy

It cannot be sufficiently emphasized that the virginity or abstinence consecrated to God presupposes
a special vocation. Virginity is not obligatory for
every Christian as is for instance the striving for
sanctity, the imitation of Christ.

Virginity presupposes a special calling, and if this
calling is not genuine, then this special self-donation
can not only lead to unbearable sufferings but can
even become an obstacle for a man's transformation
in Christ. It often happens that young men who are

ardent but do not possess holy sobriety imagine that they are called to this extraordinary sacrifice. It takes a special calling to make this sacrifice. Whether a man really has this calling is something which cannot be carefully enough tested by the man himself and by the bishop who takes him into his diocese. The same applies to the vocation to the priesthood. A man must be specially called to it and not just attracted — such attraction is all that is required in order to take up many other professions. Someone may doubt whether he has enough talent to become a musician or a painter. And whoever wants to become a philosopher should ask himself, not only whether he has enough talent, but also whether he has a real love of truth and desires only to find it, whether he is not just looking for an opportunity to develop his intellectual sharpness and agility, or to become famous and influential. In the case of many artistic and intellectual professions one should carefully test one's motives to see whether they are right or not. But in the case of the priesthood and the virginity or abstinence consecrated to God we are dealing with a vocation in a completely different sense — with a call from God, which cannot be compared with anything else. Although the calling to the priesthood and the calling to the renunciation of marriage for the sake of the kingdom of heaven are two different callings, they are nevertheless both sacred vocations in the same sense. In both a calling is present which is formally different from any other responsible and important worldly profession. This calling is such that one not only has to see whether any false motives are drawing one to the priesthood, but also whether one is being called inwardly, whether a unique call from God is present. In the case of celibacy the greatness of the sacrifice must be clearly seen and one's strength in this respect must be soberly measured. In the case of the priesthood one must see the responsibility which goes with it and which is incomparable with all other professions, as well as the sacral character of this office and of everything which goes with it. In the case of the virginity consecrated to God there must be present a deep desire for this form of dying to oneself out of love for Jesus — the depth and greatness and beauty of this sacrifice must be fully understood; and in the case of the priesthood there must be present the desire to serve God as his priest, and a deep understanding for the sublime dignity and sacred mission of the priest, for everything implied by the words of Jesus to Peter, "Feed my lambs": offering the sacrifice of the Mass, absolving sinners, administering the sacraments, tending to the needs of souls.

One speaks of both of these callings as charismas[12] and rightly so, for they presuppose a special gift of God's grace — something which is not granted to us in sanctifying grace. It takes an extraordinary gift of grace to fulfil, in a way pleasing to God, everything involved in the sacred office of the priest, or in the case of celibacy, to be able to live this sacrifice in a fruitful way pleasing to God.

Now that we have discussed at some length the nature of the priesthood and of celibacy, we are ready to turn to the affinity between the two. This will be the task of the next chapter.

NOTES

1. Dietrich von Hildebrand, *Marriage* (New York, Longmans, Green, and Co., 1959), p. 2.

2. Michael Chinigo, ed., *The Pope Speaks* (Pantheon, 1957).

3. *Ibid.*

4. *Ibid.*

5. Roger Schutz, prior of Taize, writes: "The words which we speak to Christ, 'I love you,' should be ratified with deeds if they are not to remain empty sounds. For his sake we should in every struggle destroy in ourselves whatever must be destroyed, even if in doing so we seem to harm ourselves temporarily. The intimacy with Christ will take away all our loneliness. We will become united with Christ and so strengthened in faith as to be able to move mountains." *Op. cit.*, p. 101.

6. Cardinal Newman has beautifully expressed this in an unpublished sermon on consecrated virginity held in 1854: "To make a single life its own end, to adopt it simply and solely for its own sake, I do not know whether such a state of life is more melancholy or more unamiable, melancholy from its unrequited desolateness and unamiable from the pride and self-esteem on which it is based.

"This is not the Virginity of the Gospel — it is not a state of independence or isolation, or dreary pride, or barren indolence, or crushed affections; man is made for sympathy, for the interchange of love, for self-denial for the sake of another dearer to him than himself. The Virginity of the

Christian soul is a marriage with Christ. . . . O transcending condescension that he should stoop to be ours in the tenderest and most endearing way — ours to love, ours to consult, ours to minister to, ours to converse with, ours to joy in. Ours so fully that it is as if he had none to think of but each of us personally. The very idea of matrimony is possession — whole possession — the husband is the wife's and no other's, and the wife is the husband's and none but his. This is to enter into the marriage bond . . . And this it is to be married to Jesus. It is to have him ours wholly, henceforth, and for ever — it is to be united to him by an indissoluble tie — it is to be his, while he is ours — it is to partake of that wonderful sacrament which unites him to his Blessed Mother on high — Dilectus meus mihi, et ego illi, qui pascitur inter lilia (I am my beloved's and my beloved is mine; he pastures his flock among the lilies, *Song of Solomon,* 6:2)." Quoted from *Newman the Oratorian,* ed. by Placid Murray, O.S.B. (Dublin, Gill and Macmillan Ltd., 1969), p. 277.

7. "The virginal life is the image of the blessed happiness which awaits us in the world to come." St. Gregory of Nyssa, *De Virginitate,* 13. Cf. Pope Paul's encyclical *"On Priestly Celibacy,"* no. 39.

8. That a person who is deeply recollected and at prayer can, if he is very tired, fall asleep, does not at all eliminate the radical difference between being deeply recollected in God — when we are no longer fully conscious of our surroundings — and sleeping. It is a weakness of human nature that we can slip from one attitude into the opposite attitude, and it is a typical misunderstanding when psychologists conclude to any essential relation between these attitudes simply on the basis of their temporal proximity, on the basis of our ability to slip from the one into the other. They have so completely lost all sense for differences of essence that they not only deduce from causal relations between for example physiological and psychic phenomena, that they are both in reality the same, they not only see causes in mere conditions; but they even want to deduce, from the mere possibility

of slipping from one attitude into the opposite attitude, the identity of these attitudes. We can fall from deep concentration into complete distraction, or we can, while being deeply moved by a great work of art, suddenly fall into an analysis of our experience — we are indeed in constant danger of slipping from depth into the periphery. It is a well known fact that precisely in deep and serious moments we can be particularly struck by something comical.

9. It is a typical danger of man to think that he is more realistic, more sober, freer from illusions when he takes mediocre forms of things for their valid forms simply because these mediocre forms occur so often. Of course there is also the danger of projecting a depth into things which they do not really have. Thus the divinization of history is today widespread and many people hear the "world-spirit" breathing in every piece of nonsense, in every empty theory which for some reason becomes popular for a certain period, in every sign of cultural decline. These people take the mere fact that something has achieved a certain historical realization, to prove that that thing is something deep and important. This danger, which is particularly widespread in Germany, is disastrous and in reality leads to nihilism — for if everything which occurs in history is deep simply because it occurs in history, then there is no longer any difference between high and low, deep and shallow, true and false, good and evil, holy and profane. But in our context, in the question of the value and importance of celibacy for the priest, the great danger is that of seeing everything a la baisse, of regarding everything as more real and more clearly knowable, the lower it ranks metaphysically. It is the attitude of the man who in his irreverent shallowness regards all great and high things as illusions, who thinks that he can see through all things. We have to think of the famous remark of Lichtenberg: if an ape could read St. Paul, he would see only other apes in the works of St. Paul.

10. Roger Schutz, prior of the Protestant monastery Taize, writes: "Belonging to Christ demands a break. Apart from marriage, the full dedication to Christ forbids all other rela-

tions of the same kind. And the break which follows from celibacy is an even greater one." *Op. cit.,* p. 99.

11. "The priest must not think that ordination makes everything easy for him and screens him once for all from every temptation or danger. Chastity is not acquired all at once but is a virtue resulting from a laborious conquest and daily affirmation. . . . In order to safeguard his chastity with all care and affirm its sublime meaning, the priest must consider clearly and calmly his position as a man exposed to spiritual warfare against the seductions of the flesh in himself and in the world, continually renewing his resolution to perfect more and more the irrevocable offering of himself which obliges him to a fidelity that is complete and loyal." "On Priestly Celibacy," para. 73.

12. But the term charisma has here a different meaning than for instance in the case of mystical graces, powers of healing, bilocation, or prophecy. For the calling to the priesthood or to the virginity consecrated to God does not have the same extraordinary character about it.

It is not our purpose to go into this theological question. We confine ourselves to mentioning that the charisma characteristic of the calling to the priesthood or to celibacy does not involve an extraordinary intervention of God as for instance when St. Paul heard the voice of Jesus on the way to Damascus.

Chapter IV
The Priesthood and Celibacy

We said above that celibacy corresponds better to the meaning and the nature of the priesthood, even though it does not belong to the nature of the priesthood and is not a sine qua non for it. We want now to try to present reasons for this and to show how unjustified is the demand for the elimination of obligatory celibacy.

Celibacy is something which for many reasons deeply corresponds to the meaning of the priesthood.

First of all, both the decision to become a priest and the decision to lead a life of celibacy grow out of the same attitude of soul: the unconditional giving of oneself to God, dwelling in the temple of God, belonging completely to the holy Church without any other earthly tie, dying to oneself. One cannot regard celibacy as an unnecessary burden for the priest. Celibacy has a deep inner affinity with the calling to be a priest, and obligatory celibacy has for many reasons a great and deep meaning for the priesthood. One cannot therefore speak as if this were a sacrifice

51

which can just as little be required of every priest as for instance the giving up of wine or of all alcoholic drinks could be required of every priest.

Nor is celibacy something which is only desirable for practical reasons, for instance, in order to give religious superiors a greater flexibility, though this too is an important point. The reasons for the high value of priestly celibacy are deeper and not only of this practical kind.

Celibacy and the way of being anchored in the world which results from marriage

The unique dignity of the office of the priest, which we tried to bring out in Chapter 2, showed us how important it is that the priest be free from many worldly ties, that he no longer be anchored in the "world."

Now marriage is not only a source of great human happiness — and in the case of deep mutual love, the greatest source of human happiness — it also imposes important obligations on both partners. I am not here thinking about the moral obligation to be faithful to one another. I am also not thinking of the indissolubility of marriage which so startled the apostles that they said to our Lord: "Is it not then better to remain unmarried?" No, I am thinking of the obligations of the husband to provide for his wife, and of the obligation of the wife to provide, in a different way, for her husband. I am thinking of the fact that the partners are obliged to provide for one another; and since most marriages are also potential families, they must also be ready, according to the consensus of marriage, to fulfil their duties as parents — to solemnly accept many obligations towards their children.

We must understand that these obligations present an obstacle for "completely belonging to the Church," for an exclusive service to souls in the name of the Church and as an organ of the Church. When St. Paul says with regard to the union of love in marriage that the married are "divided," his words apply particularly to the division which results from the duties which are indissolubly linked with marriage. There are countless situations where these duties could come into conflict with the duties of the priest. The priest should at all times possess perfect freedom so that he can represent the Church "in season, out of season," so that he can reproach as soon as God is offended, so that he can intervene to help those suffering injustice. In a word he should be ready to take all sacrifices upon himself. But when he is married he is obliged to consider the welfare of his wife and children. He can and should take upon himself the crosses which come from exercising his office in a way pleasing to God. But can he do this when these crosses affect his wife and children just as much as himself? As long as we are speaking of the obligation of every Catholic to suffer anything rather than to

sin and to offend God, then of course no obligation
to wife or children, no concern for their earthly welfare can in any way mitigate this primary obligation.
But should one enter into the great and solemn obligations deriving from the high office of the priest, and
at the same time enter into the obligations deriving
from marriage? Even though, as must always be emphasized, celibacy does not belong to the very nature
of the priesthood, it indisputably corresponds better
to the spirit and the meaning of the priesthood to
remain unmarried and free from all the obligations
which are indissolubly connected with marriage.

One cannot deny that the priest, because of all the
duties of marriage, can be very limited in proclaiming the word of God, in refusing to make any compromises.[1]

The unmarried priest can take all sacrifices upon
himself, even poverty and persecution, if these are
the unavoidable consequences of making no compromises. This is much more difficult for him when
he also has to expose his wife and children to the
same sacrifices. He is "divided" by the consideration
which he has to take of their welfare — he is no
longer free to live exclusively for his holy office.
One should not make the objection that in the case
of a conflict every Christian should prefer to remain
faithful to Christ than to provide for the welfare of
wife and children. Of course all laymen are obliged
to suffer martyrdom rather than to deny God, even

if this means that wife and children would die as martyrs. But the great difference is that the priest has to preach the word of God ex officio, because of the office he holds, that he should raise his voice like St. John the Baptist when an influential public personality gives public scandal by his sins. In remaining silent when he should speak the priest not only compromises himself, but also in a certain sense the Church, for instance as pastor in the eyes of his parishioners.

Celibacy is not comparable with the voluntary poverty* of a priest

Many say that they do not deny that celibacy is more adequate to the priesthood, they only say that this fact does not justify *obligatory* priestly celibacy. They point out that it is more beautiful and edifying when a priest lives in great poverty, as the Curé of Ars did, but this is not imposed upon every priest, one does not oblige everyone who feels himself called to the priesthood to take a vow of poverty.

This argumentation rests upon a great error. The priest remains unmarried not as an edifying ascetical practice but to be free from the obligations imposed by marriage. If a priest is wealthy, if he leads a luxurious life instead of helping others with his money, this is a regrettable mistake. But if he lives modestly yet not in poverty, he does nothing wrong — but he has not chosen the heroic imitation of Christ which deeply edifies us in the Curé of Ars. Possessions may be a temptation for him and threaten to make him "worldly." He remains exposed to the danger of worldly interests.

Wealth is certainly a temptation to forget what the sacred office of the priest imposes, a temptation of getting involved in worldly cares — but the concern for one's possessions is not an obligation[2] willed by God as is the concern for wife and children in marriage. But if the priest could marry, he would not only be exposed to the danger of being drawn into worldly affairs, but he would take upon himself a holy obligation toward his wife and whatever children he would have, and this would hinder him from being completely only an instrument of the Church, from totally living for his office as priest.

In the case of possessions it is the danger of worldliness which can present a conflict with the priesthood. In the case of marriage it is the conflict of the duties of a husband and a father with those of the priesthood. The first type of conflict, the danger of worldliness, can appear in very different forms. Every Christian and especially every priest is called upon to fight against it. One cannot prevent it from without by any laws — but every Christian must constantly fight against it. In the case of marriage it is not a question of the danger of worldliness, but rather of assuming duties which one must not neglect but which collide with exclusive dedication to the holy work of the priest, which at least make it more difficult for him to devote himself to his holy office freely and without hindrance.

Marriage is not only the most intimate natural union of love, it is also a formal community. It involves rights of the marriage partners and is in a certain sense anchored in the state — although it is in no way a part of the state but goes far beyond this sphere. In a word even marriage has a juridical structure. Marriage is also the basis for the family and, as already mentioned, every marriage can become a family. In marrying one takes all kinds of obligations upon oneself, even obligations towards the children which may result from the marriage. This whole juridical aspect of marriage shows clearly the advantage which the celibate priest has over the married priest. The legal ties deriving from marriage are inappropriate to the function[3] of the priest as an instrument of the church. These ties force him into a position in life which puts him on a level with all laymen and which endangers the unique freedom which he should possess as someone belonging totally to the Church. It is a great advantage for the priest, who speaks to souls in the name of God, who represents the holy Church, who shows in his sacred office what it means "to be not of this world," it is a great advantage for him to be separated, in a way for all to see, from the world by the absence of the ties deriving from marriage.

Obligatory celibacy can therefore clearly not be compared with obligatory priestly poverty.

It is hard to understand that a believing Catholic who loves the holy Church could fail to see the glorious freedom which celibacy bestows upon the priest. Is it not a wonderful thing that the bearer of the sacred office of the priest, the man who has been given the power of consecration, who administers the sacraments and proclaims the word of God, is freed by celibacy from all ties to this world, belongs exclusively to the Church, and is clearly separated from the rest of society? Is it not wonderful that there is such a thing? And can one overlook that celibacy is for many reasons far more adequate to the priesthood than marriage?

Should the great sacrifice of celibacy be obligatory for every priest?

The fact that celibacy imposes personal sacrifices on the priest is no argument for eliminating obligatory celibacy, for we are here dealing, not with earthly things, but with something deriving its meaning and justification exclusively from the reality of the supernatural, with an office which does not, like some government position, depend for its meaning on the structure of earthly life, but which has dignity, validity, value only if the holy Church was founded by Christ, the Son of God.

Arguments such as "Many priests suffer under it"

are unsound. Crosses and sacrifices are unavoidable for every Christian. The suffering resulting from a profession for which one is unsuited is a general fact of life. The solemn and indissoluble tie to another person in marriage can turn out to be a terrible chain and a heavy cross. To be a priest yet without having the vocation is a terrible burden. This also applies to celibacy.

The duty of Church authorities to test vocations very carefully

But from this one can only conclude that the decision to become a priest cannot be made seriously enough, nor can the church authorities be careful enough in determining whether in a given case a vocation really is present. This has certainly not always been the case.[4] The fear of having too few priests can present the great temptation of being satisfied with too little, of demanding too little from the candidates. One often represented marriage to seminarians in as negative a light as possible so as to make it easier for them to choose celibacy. For the same reason one sometimes spoke very negatively to the seminarians about women so as to turn them against women. These are great and irresponsible mistakes and the results can be disastrous. But obligatory celibacy is not responsible for these results; they rather come from the failure to make the subdeacon realize what it is that he is giving up for the sake of the kingdom of heaven. In failing to show him marriage in the most beautiful light, one fails to help him to take the vow of consecrated virginity with full consciousness of what he is giving up.

But unfortunately the so-called progressivists give a false response to this failure. As happens so often, one reacts by falling into a false alternative. One thinks it necessary to introduce the seminarian or theology student to a worldly or even an impure atmosphere so that he can know what he is giving up in leading a life of celibacy. One thinks that he need not keep the distance from the sexual sphere which every Christian should keep before marriage. One fails to see that from the moment he decides to become a priest he should keep a special holy distance[5] from the sensual sphere and should avoid any contact with the female sex as soon as the least sensual note enters into a relation. For him to understand the reality, the beauty, the depth of the mystery of the sensual sphere and its purpose and fulfilment in the mutual self-donation of marriage, for him to understand what he is giving up, he does not have to be exposed to isolated sensuality, nor encouraged to have contacts with the other sex which are too familiar and irreverent. This is one of the many false reactions in the Church today. One thinks that the error of treating the sensual sphere and marriage as somehow taboo can be corrected by subtly destroying in the seminarians all reverence for this sphere and for marriage — this is done by sending them to impure movies, letting them read impure books, in a word by submerging them in an impure world or else in a world in which the mystery character of this sphere is destroyed, in which the sensual sphere is represented as a purely neutral biological sphere. One poses the false alternative: either regard the sensual sphere as taboo, or revel in Venusberg for a while — or, what is worse, neutralize the whole sensual sphere of marriage, represent it as merely a healthy biological instinct. This latter is a real castration, an "emasculation," far more than were the earlier taboos with regard to this sphere.

Only when the subdeacon sees in their highest light, in their true, authentic form the mystery of the sensual sphere, the sublime communion of love in marriage, which Christ has raised to a sacrament, the still more sublime sealing off of the sensual sphere for the sake of the kingdom of heaven which follows from renouncing marriage, which is the greatest source of earthly happiness, only then is the subdeacon in a position to make a fully free decision for celibacy, to be conscious of all the sacrifices which this involves but also of the unspeakable gift of a unique union with Christ.[6] Only then will the subdeacon clearly understand that celibacy corresponds better to the meaning and nature of the priesthood, that it is more adequate for the priest, and that obligatory celibacy is a precious gift for the priest.

NOTES

1. Even though this no longer plays the role which it did at the time of Pope St. Gregory VII, still prevailing political trends could lead one to make compromises for the sake of one's children. This is an even greater danger in the countries behind the Iron Curtain, and was a great danger in Nazi Germany.

2. When we say that possessions impose no obligations as does marriage, we of course do not mean that the priest is not obliged to avoid waste in managing his money, and to help needy persons with what remains after providing for his own necessities. He can turn over to a trustworthy friend who is knowledgable in these things the task of investing his money carefully. And we are not here thinking about priests who have great wealth — a rare case — but rather about the difference between holy poverty and comfortable means. What we said above becomes clearer here: comfortable means may contain a temptation to worldliness, but the priest has no obligation towards them — except for the general obligation not to waste them, which is replaced by the other obligation not to lead a luxurious life. But he has no obligation to his money as a husband has to his wife.

3. Cf. my book *Metaphysik der Gemeinschaft* (Regensburg, 1955), Part III, Chapters 2 and 4.

4. "In fact the responsibility falls not on consecrated celibacy in itself but on a judgment of the fitness of the candidate for the priesthood which was not always adequate or prudent or prompt enough, or else it falls on the way in which sacred ministers live unworthily of their life of total consecration." "On Priestly Celibacy," para. 83.

5. "The young candidates for the priesthood should convince themselves that they are not able to follow their difficult way without a special type of asceticism which is more demanding than that which is asked of all the other faithful and which is proper to themselves as candidates for the priesthood. We are speaking of an asceticism which is demanding but not suffocating, which consists in the deliberate and assiduous practice of those virtues which distinguish a

priest from other men: self-denial in the highest degree —
an essential for following Christ (cf. Mt. 16, 24; Jn. 12, 25).
"On Priestly Celibacy," para. 70.

6. "Once moral certainty has been obtained that the
maturity of the candidate is sufficiently guaranteed, he will
be in a position to take on himself the heavy and sweet
burden of sacerdotal chastity as a total gift of himself to
the Lord and to His Church. . . . in that solemn moment
when the candidate will decide once and for his whole life,
he will not feel the weight of an imposition from without,
but rather the interior joy that accompanies a choice made
for the love of Christ." "On Priestly Celibacy," para. 72.

Chapter V

The Special Importance of Celibacy in the Present Situation

Obligatory celibacy is not only, as we just saw, more adequate to the meaning and nature of the priesthood; it takes on today a special importance in the present crisis in the Church: it is a good obstacle for many who would choose the priesthood without really having the vocation to it.

Former false motives for becoming a priest

There were always men who were drawn to the priesthood because of the authority proper to this office or because of the social position which it gave the priest. Some men were also drawn by the guarantee of a certain amount of economic security. Whereas this guarantee has been absent in France since the beginning of this century (and absent in Italy even longer) and has actually been replaced by the prospect of considerable poverty for the priest (unless his family is wealthy), it is still present in for instance Germany and America. In these countries a certain economic ease has been guaranteed to the secular priest whether he is a pastor in a parish or an assistant or a teacher in a Catholic school or editor of a magazine. The authority and social position of the priest can be a point of attraction to the priesthood in all countries, especially for men from the lower classes such as sons of farmers and laborers, for upon becoming priests they automatically enter a higher social class. In reality the priesthood raises a man above all differences of class; his office is so far above all worldly considerations that he is beyond all class differences and social circles. But for this reason he has access to all levels of society. Back when class differences still played a great role, the priest was accepted in every salon as someone who naturally fitted in — except in non-Catholic countries where his priesthood made him suspect for very different reasons. The son of a farmer or a laborer in entering the priesthood became an "educated man," he became someone clearly raised above the farming or working class. This did not hinder him from feeling a great solidarity with the workers or farmers, or from becoming an apostle to the poor. We are here speaking of rising to a higher class in the eyes of society.

Of course sons of farmers or workers could in special cases rise in society thanks to special talents; they could become professors, doctors, lawyers, statesmen, industrialists, just as they could become rich for different reasons. But these were exceptions requiring special talents or at least special luck. Of course this illegitimate motivation for choosing the priesthood is today less common since it is much easier to rise in society and since practically everyone goes to college.

False motives for becoming a priest today

But another danger has become much greater today. Another illegitimate motive for choosing the priesthood, a motive radically contradicting the true vocation to it, has become common today which was not present earlier. Until recently the priest was aware that in instructing, in his pastoral duties, in proclaiming the word of God he had to adhere strictly to the teaching of the Church, to the deposit of the Catholic faith. Ever since Pope Pius X the oath against modernism has made every priest understand clearly that in teaching and acting he is obliged to follow, not his own private interpretation of the Christian revelation, not the modernist theories of any theologian, but exclusively the deposit of the Catholic faith. But today, in this "revolution" within the Church, the course of studies in many seminaries does not present the deposit of the Catholic faith as the absolute and unchangeable truth, but presents the most various heresies as well. Many theologians call for pluralism in the magisterium of the Church and in sermons one constantly hears things in radical contradiction to the teaching of the Church and the dogmas. More and more the priest believes that he can follow his own inclinations and ideas *without* losing his authority with the laity, an authority which he has *only* as representative of the Church. Whereas earlier, as soon as he opposed the teaching of the Church and spread heresies he was disciplined and, if he did not obey, was relieved of his office, today this usually does not take place so easily and thus he retains in the eyes of the laity his authority as an official representative of the Church. Thus he can indulge all his personal sympathies and dubious religious speculations (or swim with the tide of the times and all its errors) and at the same time can enjoy an authority which he has in reality undermined, or to put it better, an authority which has become illusory.[1]

This is tremendously attractive for many — a unique opportunity to bestow a great importance and a pseudo-authority upon *their* ideas, which are usually just a mindless repetition of fashionable slogans. Since we live in a time in which a pseudo-apostolate is especially widespread, in which everyone wants to play the prophet, in which counseling and guidance have become a passion, the authority of the priest is particularly appealing. Without adhering to the directives of the Church he can use the authority of the Church in his role as counselor and leader. When the Holy Father condemns artificial birth-control, he feels justified in telling people in confession or those under his guidance what he, despite the position of the Pope, thinks is right; but those going to confession to him continue to hear in him the voice of the Church. We need not dwell any longer on this attraction which the priesthood possesses for many in the present grave crisis in the Church, an attraction separated by an abyss from the true vocation to the priesthood.

Obligatory celibacy as a good test of genuine vocations

The important thing to see is that all these illegitimate motives usually do not suffice to motivate a man to take upon himself the sacrifice of abstinence and the renunciation of marriage. As long as obligatory celibacy remains in effect it is probable that men who are drawn to the priesthood not by a true calling to it but by such illegitimate motives, will shrink back from taking upon themselves such a sacrifice. Thus obligatory celibacy is today a good test for the presence of a true vocation, of complete dedication to Christ, of the readiness to take up the cross.

One could object: but in the Eastern Church where there is no obligatory celibacy, this test is absent, yet without causing any harm. To this objection we answer that this attraction to the priesthood from false motives is not nearly so great there. Especially the situation of those behind the iron curtain imposes countless heavy sacrifices upon priests, and thus East and West are not comparable.

**The special importance of celibacy today and the
shortage of priests**

Another objection is that, because of the prevailing
state of mind today, the general desire to remove the
cross and all sacrifice from the Church, and especially
because of the secularization and the disappearance
of real faith, we will have a shortage of priests if
obligatory celibacy is not abolished. This is Karl
Rahner's position in his letter on celibacy (in which
he says many beautiful and important things about
celibacy and in favor of the appropriateness of obligatory celibacy): if obligatory celibacy really should
lead to a shortage of priests, then it must of course
be abolished.

The question which must be raised here is: is it
a greater evil to have too few priests than to have
many who do not have a real calling to the priesthood?

Here we must refer back to our earlier discussion
of the new situation in the Church which has arisen
as a result of the crisis in the Church. There were
always priests who fell with regard to abstinence, as
well as priests who in their mediocrity and indifference were not equal to their mission as priests. This
is an unavoidable display of human weakness. It
cannot be prevented. But the above-mentioned danger
of pastors and teachers abusing the authority which
the office of the priest bestows in order to spread
teachings radically opposed to the deposit of the

Catholic faith, creates a situation in which the shortage of priests is a lesser evil than the existence of
priests who are only in appearance representatives
of the Church. Is it not better to have too few doctors than to have many who are in reality charlatans
but who appear before the public with the authority
of a real doctor! And the shortage of doctors can
bring it about that many lose their lives as a result
of receiving no medical help. In the case of the
shortage of priests there is the danger that in certain
places holy Mass will only rarely be celebrated, that
many children will not receive religious instruction,
that many will die without the sacraments. That is certainly a great evil — but it does not have to be fatal
for the souls of the faithful. For parents can instruct
their children in the elements of the faith (this often
happened in times of persecution). Souls can be
saved by perfect contrition when they cannot receive
the sacraments before dying. But the spreading of
false teachings by those who are in the eyes of the
laity the voice of the Church is incomparably more
terrible. When one considers the shortage of priests
in the present situation a greater evil than the activity
of a priest who is no longer the obedient son of the
Church and who, what is worse, no longer professes
the teaching of the magisterium of the Church in
faith and morals, then one has lost the supernatural
understanding of the Church. This would indeed be
a truly negative legalism, as opposed to the Church's

promulgation of moral commandments which is often erroneously branded "legalism."

Thus today more than ever the sacrifice involved in celibacy is a good test for the true faith and thus a considerable guarantee for the real calling to the priesthood. And besides, the great decline (which has already begun) of vocations to the priesthood is not primarily a result of obligatory celibacy but rather of the triumph of secularization and the disappearance of the supernatural spirit.[2] If the Church has for 2000 years erroneously interpreted the Christian Revelation and if faith in the supernatural character of the Church was an illusion, how can anyone from legitimate motives want to become a priest? It becomes on the other hand more difficult for those who are really called, to decide to enter the seminary, when they run the risk of losing their faith there.

It is undoubtedly better that there be fewer priests than priests who destroy the faith. If a bad priest was able to do great damage and to lead souls away from the Church and the faith, the danger to souls today is much greater in being exposed to priests who are not "bad" but heretical, who replace faith in Christ by various modern myths. The bad priest is recognized as bad, he gives scandal and the laity backs away from him. They realize what a priest should be and what the Church expects from a true priest and they are indignant at him for not living up to this. The bad priests *forfeit* their authority.

But the modern teachers of error give no scandal for many. They retain their authority in the eyes of the laity and the laity thus lets itself be poisoned out of obedience to the Church. This damage to souls is incomparably greater. They are deceived and receive poison into their souls which they mistake for the spiritual nourishment offered to them by the Church. They let themselves be unwittingly defrauded of their faith. This same priest is perhaps helpful and friendly, perhaps even kind to them, he gives no scandal by an immoral life, and thus he becomes a wolf in sheep's clothing. The "bad" priest was a wolf in wolf's clothing. Thus obligatory celibacy takes on today an even greater importance than at the time of Pope St. Gregory VII.

Obligatory celibacy is not only more adequate to the office of priest, as we saw; it also possesses another high value, and far from being outdated today, it is even today an invaluable test for the presence of the true vocation to the priesthood.[3]

NOTES

1. Kierkegaard has written on the subject of the authority of the priest: "The Christian discourse deals in a certain measure with doubt — the sermon functions absolutely, solely and only, by means of authority, that of the Scriptures and of the apostles of Christ. It is therefore absolute heresy to deal in sermons with doubt, even if one knows ever so well how to handle it. . . . The sermon implies the priest (and ordination); the Christian discourse can be delivered by the ordinary man." Quoted by Walter Lowrie, *Kierke-*

gaard (Torch Books, Harper and Row, New York), vol. I, p. 274.

2. "It is simply not possible to believe that the abolition of ecclesiastical celibacy would considerably increase the number of priestly vocations: the contemporary experience of those churches . . . which allow their ministers to marry seems to prove the contrary. The cause of the decrease in vocations to the priesthood is to be found elsewhere, especially for example, in the fact that individuals and families have lost their sense of God and of all that is holy and their esteem for the Church as the institution of salvation through faith and sacraments . . . " "On Priestly Celibacy," para. 49.

3. One might object: how can it be a test when celibacy does not belong to the very nature of the priesthood, when the vocation to the priesthood does not necessarily include the vocation to celibacy?

We respond by saying that under certain circumstances something can be the test for the true vocation to the priesthood even though it does not belong to the nature of the priesthood. For certain things can test whether someone is called to marry someone else, though without belonging to the nature of marriage. Many marry for financial reasons. If one partner has no wealth, this motive drops away. This of course does not mean that if both are rich they cannot marry for pure love, nor that if both are poor they must be marrying for love. But still one often tested the motivation of a man seeking to marry a rich girl, by telling him that she had lost all her money. In a similar way obligatory celibacy is a good test for the absence of false motives, or for the presence of a true vocation. Of course if someone belonging to a religious order said that he did not want to take the vow of abstinence and did not want to renounce marriage, he would crassly contradict himself. Celibacy belongs so necessarily to life in a religious order that a married man who wanted to be a monk at the same time would be a contradictio in adjecto (self-contradiction).

As emphasized above celibacy does not in this way belong to the very nature of the priesthood. But that does not alter the fact that the readiness to make this great sacrifice is a sign that the true vocation to the priesthood is present, it does not alter the fact that the man possessing this readiness is under present-day conditions far less likely to seek the priesthood out of false motives. Of course the calling to abstinence and to remaining unmarried for the sake of the kingdom of heaven is not sufficient for the calling to the priesthood. Someone can be called to be a lay brother in an order and thus be called to celibacy yet not to the priesthood. This is even more the case for women who live a life of consecrated virginity in a convent or in the world.

Chapter VI

The Misuse of the Words "Voluntary" and "Obligatory" in the Discussion on Celibacy

What those opposing obligatory celibacy really want is that the decision for or against celibacy be left up to the individual who feels himself called to the priesthood. Most of them see celibacy as something positive, but as an heroic sacrifice which must be voluntarily chosen by the individual and must not be required of him.

But the word voluntary in this context contains an equivocation.

1. "Voluntary" as the opposite of force from without

First of all the word voluntary can refer to the opposite of all force from without. The state forces us to pay taxes, and in most countries the male youth is forced to spend a year or two in the military service. Parents are forced by the state to send their children to school. None of this is voluntary. Whether someone wants to do these things or not, he is punished for not doing them.

77

2. "Voluntary" as the opposite of morally obligatory

The words voluntary and involuntary take on a completely different meaning in referring to moral obligations. These are not obligatory in the sense of a force from without, for they appeal explicitly to our free consent. They call upon us to realize our deepest freedom, our moral freedom, which is the fulfilment of our ontological freedom, or our freedom of will. But the obligation of moral obligations is far deeper, incomparably more important (than obligation in the first sense above). They are absolute and categorical; they are unchangeable; they transcend the earthly sphere. Man can refuse to obey them — but he ought not.

The act in which we obey a moral call and thus obey God is voluntary in the deepest sense of the word and radically opposed to all force from without. But this act is obligatory and is not "voluntary" as are heroic moral deeds or decisions such as all forms of strict asceticism, or the saving of the life of another at the risk of losing one's own, or all sacrifices and especially the evangelical counsels. Since we are not obliged to do these things they are voluntary in a completely new sense.

3. "Voluntary" in the sense of being able to ignore the obligations which one has freely taken upon oneself

The second meaning of voluntary refers to the absence of a moral obligation. But voluntary in this sense does not mean that if we have voluntarily bound ourselves to do things which are in themselves not obligatory, we are free to ignore or to give up these voluntarily accepted obligations if for some reason we do not want to fulfil them.

Celibacy is voluntary because neither external force nor moral obligation compels one to bind oneself to celibacy

The meaning of voluntary as the opposite of external force is emphasized in the teaching of the Church. A moral action must be done freely, in free obedience, and not under external compulsion. Whoever does not freely submit to the call of a morally relevant good and to the command of God contained in it but acts under compulsion or from fear of unpleasant natural consequences, deprives his action thereby of all moral value.

The Church also emphasizes that all freely accepted obligations must be voluntary in the sense of the opposite of external force.

If someone marries under pressure and was not free in consenting, this marriage is invalid and his lack of freedom is grounds for annulment. The choice of the priesthood must also be voluntary, that is, free from external pressure — if the choice can be shown to have been made under pressure, this is a sufficient reason for laicizing the priest at his request and releasing him from celibacy. Thus, it is misleading for those advocating the abolition of obligatory celibacy in the Latin Church to say: celibacy must be voluntarily chosen, we cannot be obliged to accept it as a moral law obliges us. This is misleading because today as at all earlier times priestly celibacy is voluntary and is imposed upon priests neither by external compulsion nor as a moral law; it is rather the case that in accepting celibacy a priest binds himself, he enters into an obligation.

Voluntary does not mean that the individual can at will separate celibacy and the priesthood

It is however not left up to us to separate celibacy and the priesthood, to become a priest in the Western Church and to reject celibacy. But this is clearly a quite new meaning of involuntary.

If it is objectively better for the priest to be celibate, if celibacy is more adequate to the meaning and nature of the priesthood, then this clearly suffices to justify the linking together of celibacy with the priesthood, as well as to justify the Church's decision to make celibacy obligatory for the priest.

One might object: celibacy involves after all great and heavy sacrifices which cannot be required by the Church; the heroic decision to make such a sacrifice must be freely made by the individual. To this we respond as follows: we have already seen that the objection to celibacy based on the great sacrifice which it involves is unsound. But now we have to see that it is false to assert: "because of the sacrifice involved it must be left up to the individual whether he will, besides the priesthood, also choose celibacy." We have to remember that the total self-donation to God involved in the office of the priest is even more demanding than celibacy. Let us consider the sexual abstinence in which married couples sometimes choose to live,[1] or the involuntary sacrifice imposed on a man or woman who because of an unhappy love is hindered from marrying; and let us compare this with the offering of his own life which the priest makes to God and to the Church (think of his great responsibility and of everything demanded of him because he has the tremendous dignity of being able to consecrate) : then we see what a shallow view of the priesthood and of its ultimate seriousness someone betrays in saying: "I would gladly take upon myself the sacrifices involved in the priesthood, but celibacy — no, that is asking too much!"

The fact that I can only have certain things when I am willing to take on certain obligations, is no limitation on my voluntariness, it is however a limitation on my arbitrariness — but to act arbitrarily is just the opposite of true freedom. If someone were to say that he did not voluntarily choose the examinations required for practicing medicine, that he wanted to be a doctor but that the examinations were imposed on him, he would clearly be equivocating with the word voluntary. The examinations do not belong to the nature of being a good doctor, they are not necessary presuppositions for this as is the required knowledge. It is a positive law of the state which requires examinations for the practice of medicine.

Celibacy should not be only an unavoidable sacrifice for the priest with a real vocation

But in the case of the priest it is even necessary that he feel a special calling to celibacy, that he not simply swallow it as an unavoidable sacrifice. The fact that the Church links celibacy with the priesthood in the Western Church is in no way a mitigation of the free choice of celibacy. The true vocation to the priesthood demands of me that I give myself totally to Christ and his holy Church and that I desire to hold this great office according to the laws of holy Church. The vocation to celibacy is thus a sign of the true vocation to the priesthood — not because it belongs to the nature of the priesthood, but because it belongs to the spirit of obedience and dedication to accept the priesthood as the Church requires hic et nunc.

The situation of the priest who wants to dissolve the obligations which he has freely taken upon himself

The situation is of course quite different when those who are already priests say that celibacy is imposed against their will because they would like to marry yet cannot. Let us suppose the most noble case: a priest meets a woman whom he loves with a deep marital love. As tragic as this conflict can be — it has nothing to do with the voluntary choosing of celibacy. It is rather a conflict between a voluntary decision to live in celibacy, a solemn voluntary bond, and an experience awakening in him the desire to break this voluntary bond. This is similar to the case of a husband who, because of the bond of marriage which he freely entered into, cannot marry another woman as long as his wife lives, however much he might love another woman, however clearly he discovers that he made a great mistake in marrying the first time, or that he has been living in illusions. But clearly no one could say that his present situation shows that he did not marry voluntarily, or that in marrying he did not clearly know how he was binding himself. The case of the priest is not as tragic, for he can sometimes be laicized and even receive permission to marry. In this case he can be given a dispensation from his solemn bond, whereas there is no dispensation from the marriage bond (unless it can be annulled on other grounds).

The greatest misuse of the word "voluntary"

Someone might object that many priests do not want to be laicized, they want to marry and remain priests. Thus celibacy is not voluntary but imposed by the Church. Here the misuse of the word voluntary comes to a climax. Such priests want to have the right to dictate to the Church according to their personal wishes, to remain as priests in the Western Church and to marry. They not only want the priesthood and celibacy to be separated in the Western Church in the future, they not only want the choice of celibacy to be always left up to the individual priest; they also want to eliminate their obligation to remain celibate which they solemnly took upon themselves before their ordination. They thus want something which is not even possible in the Eastern Church, where the priest may indeed marry before ordination, but never after. Here we cannot help asking: which priests desire this? How do the priests who demand this exercise their high office? Are they priests who really want to serve God with fear and trembling, who burn with zeal for the spreading of the kingdom of Christ, who possess the full *sentire cum ecclesia* and a deeply reverent spirit of obedience toward the Church — or are they priests who see their priestly duties as lying primarily in social action and who have lost their sense of the supernatural?[2] It follows from everything that we have said that one must suppose that they are these latter priests. They want to remain priests for many natural reasons which make their office agreeable to them — reasons which we discussed above in discussing the false motives for seeking the priesthood. Those who want to be laicized and to marry at least take upon themselves the humiliation of clearly having been unequal to their high office. However sad their failure, there is at least something positive in their implicit admission of failure. This is quite different from the case of the priest who marries without ecclesiastical permission, who thus leaves the Church, and who, usually as a form of self-defense, becomes an enemy of the Church. But worst of all is in a certain sense the case of the priest who does not want to give up his office but who does want to marry and who, because this is refused him, says that the Church has imposed upon his freedom.

So we see how badly misused the word "voluntary" is in the propaganda for the abolition of obligatory celibacy.[3]

It is the Church which lays down the conditions for the priesthood

But above all people forget that the priest gives his life not only to Christ but also to his holy Church. His life belongs to the holy Church, he works in her and through her and his work in the vineyard of the Lord is performed in the name of the Church. He receives the ordination to the priesthood from the hands of the Church. And so he has to leave it up to the authority of the Church to lay down the conditions for holding the office of the priest.

NOTES

1. In German there is a special term for such a marriage: *Josefsehe,* that is, a "marriage like that of St. Joseph."

2. Jean Cardinal Daniélou said in a speech held during a recent visit in Washington: "The Church should not accommodate herself to the modern world. She must fill with new life the religious life of all peoples." "If the Church

does not bring God to the modern world, then she has lost her raison d'etre." "We do not need the Church to create a social order. The main mission of the Church today is to remind men that the Church belongs not to a social but to a supernatural order."

3. It is a quite different case when married Protestant ministers convert and want to be ordained as priests. Before their conversion they felt themselves to be ministers and proclaimers of the word of God, and it is understandable that, after they have discovered the Catholic Church as the true Church of Christ, they have the desire to become priests. One can rightly suppose that they are seeking the priesthood for right reasons. On the other hand they have been married for years, and it would not only be a great sacrifice to separate from their wives or at least to live with them as brother and sister; this would actually contradict their duties toward their wives. There were cases in the pontificate of Pius XII where such married ministers were made priests after converting. But this is a great exception and presupposes special circumstances. These priests need in no way be in favor of abolishing obligatory celibacy. On the contrary they undoubtedly have great understanding for the value of obligatory celibacy, but they are reverently grateful for the extraordinary gift of being able to solve in this way the conflict deriving from the bonds into which they entered before their conversion.

On this subject Pope Paul VI wrote: "On the other hand, a study may be allowed of the particular circumstances of married sacred ministers of churches or other Christian communities separated from the Catholic communion, and of the possibility of admitting to priestly functions those who desire to adhere to the fullness of this communion and to continue to exercise the sacred ministry. The circumstances must be such, however, as not to prejudice the existing discipline regarding celibacy." "On Priestly Celibacy," para. 42.

Chapter VII
Difference and Unity of Priests and Laity

The argument that priests form a separate "caste"; the organic structure of communities

The assertion, sometimes made by those advocating the abolition of obligatory celibacy,[1] that celibacy separates priests from the laity into a kind of "caste," is in many respects particularly unfortunate.

They seem to think that every organic structure within human society has to lead unavoidably to a division. Even on a natural level this is a complete error. If one tries to extend equality beyond the sphere of certain fundamental rights, human society becomes an atomized mass. It loses all differentiation, and all deep human relations are leveled and deprived of their particular character. In this way all of human community is laid waste and turned into a desert of boredom. The family shows clearly that the relation of the parents to the children and that of the children to the parents must and should be different. Precisely this difference is necessary for the specific unity of the family. This difference does

87

not separate the children from their parents but rather unites them in a deep way. It is analogous in the relation between a teacher and his students, between disciple and master, between the young and their elders. In trying to reduce all human relations to the level of a kind of camaraderie one destroys their wealth and the depth.

If this is the case even on the natural level, it is incomparably more the case in the supernatural community of the holy Church. The hierarchic structure has here a great value and belongs essentially to this community. The difference between ecclesia docens (the teaching Church) and ecclesia discens (the listening Church) on the one hand, between laity and priests on the other, the difference between priest and bishop, and finally between the bishops and the bishop of Rome, the vicar of Christ on earth — all these differences do not divide but rather unite in a way appropriate to the meaning and the nature of this community.

The fundamental "sameness" of all members of the Church and the variety of offices

Of course there is also here the community of all living members of the mystical body of Christ, in which all are equal except insofar as some distinguish themselves from others by their personal sanctity. But this "sameness" of all members of the mystical body of Christ is in no way opposed to the

hierarchy of offices just mentioned. Apart from seeing how basically false the thesis is that all hierarchy
and inequality divides, we must also see with regard
to the relation between priest and laity that it is essential for the sacred character of the priesthood
and for the priest's function as minister of the sacraments and as pastor of souls, that laymen look up
to the priest with deep reverence because of his sacred
office and that they not approach him as a kind of
buddy (to say nothing of approaching him as 'frère
et cochon'). A layman should never look upon a
priest only as a good friend who can help him and
advise him. For one can regard someone as a friend
only on the basis of his individual character, his personality, not on the basis of his office; and if the
friendship with and the trust in another person which
is based on his individual character is in one respect
a deeper community, then the reverence for and the
trust in a priest which is based on his sacred supernatural office is something quite new and reaches
into a depth of the soul which is otherwise not actualized. History as well as the experience which every
individual Catholic has had shows clearly that the
truly religious layman wants the priest to be different
and to be free from worldly ties and that he trusts
the priest precisely because of this difference and
freedom. But if the priest is not set apart from the
community by virtue of his office but is only a social
figure like the doctor or judge or teacher, if in other

words he is only one among many, this undermines a sound and fruitful relation between him and the laity and destroys deep religious-supernatural community between them. Simply the lively faith that the power of consecration has been entrusted to the priest, that he represents Christ at the altar, should fill the laity with deep reverence and should exclude all chuminess and familiarity in their contact with him. Everything which accentuates this sacred character of the position of the priest is a blessing and will further his true mission, his apostolate, and help him bear fruit in the souls of the laity.

The danger of pontificalism is no argument against the hierarchy in the Church

Of course everything can be perverted. The priest is a man and is exposed to dangers just as every layman is. His high office may seduce him to a proud enjoying of his dignity instead of awakening in him a deep humility, instead of making him tremble at the sacred dignity of his office which he so little deserves, instead of making him feel like an "unprofitable servant." He may assume a "pontifical" attitude, by which he falls into a purely natural, secularized caste mentality. But the possibility of abuse is never grounds for judging the value of a thing. Every profession, every situation, every position, every relationship with other men runs the danger of abuse, perversion, distortion. The devil is the ape of God. Should all authority be eliminated simply because it can be abused? Should democracy be abolished simply because we encounter an abuse of it every day? Should marriage be abolished because there are so many unhappy marriages?

Secularization and desacralization as the reason for the "officialdom" in the Church

Ironically enough it is forgotten by those who blame celibacy for separating priests into a "caste" which looks down upon the laity, that such a class can form only when priests lose their full sense of the supernatural. They fall into a pontifical attitude because they no longer understand the sacred, supernatural character of their office, which requires the clear consciousness, on the one hand, of how little they deserve the dignity of their office, and on the other hand, of how great their responsibility before God is. It is not by obscuring the difference between priest and laity — which contradicts the meaning and nature of the priesthood — that priests are protected from this mistake, but rather by emphasizing the supernatural character of the priestly office, by avoiding all secularization, by strengthening the sense for the supernatural. It is this spirit which leads the man who bears the highest priestly dignity, the vicar of Christ on earth, to call himself *servus servorum,* "servant of servants."

To reject celibacy because it emphasizes the difference between priest and laity too much and thus supposedly "divides," is to betray that the real motive for struggling to abolish obligatory celibacy is the terrible secularization of our time, the blindness for the sacred character of the priesthood. This is the same spirit which sees the priesthood as one natural profession among others and which thus demands the right of priests to form unions.

If it were true that celibacy separates the priest from the laity in the sense of reducing the trust of the laity in the priest and even of repelling the laity,[2] then the relation to the priest in the Eastern Church or in the orthodox church should be a much closer one than in the Roman Church. But this is by no means the case, just the contrary: there the people look up particularly to the religious orders (whose members are celibates) — think of the role of the Staretz in Russia.

It is altogether characteristic that the priests urging the abolition of obligatory celibacy are the very ones striving to desacralize the Church and the priesthood. They have lost all understanding for the sacredness of the priesthood. Their ideal is not only to obscure the difference between priest and laity but above all to obscure the difference between the priesthood and other professions. They consider it as an interference in their human and civil rights when they cannot as in other professions form into groups on the model of trade unions, when they cannot regard their relation to their bishops in the light of a worldly contract, when they cannot abolish as undemocratic the obedience which they owe them and replace it by the obedience which any subordinate in a worldly organization owes his superiors as a result of his contract.

Curiously enough these priests who constantly rail against the legalism in the Church do not realize that in desacralizing the priesthood they reduce the priest to a mere official of the Church. They fail to understand that legalism and secularization are intimately related.

There were always sects such as the Albigensians, Joachim of Flora, etc., who opposed every form and every juridical structure in the Church and wanted to replace these by the so-called purely charismatic church. But what they were striving for was rather a Church stripped of all authority and all forms; their ideal was a kind of religious "bohème." But today's enemies of the "institutional Church," those who oppose as legalism the obligatory celibacy for priests (as distinguished from the celibacy freely chosen by the individual priest), are striving to assimilate the priesthood to other, non-sacred professions and in reality to make the priest bourgeois — they thus introduce a legalistic spirit.

It is the special privilege of the priest to concentrate on the "one thing necessary," to consider all the things of the world in the light of Christ and of eternity, to which we are called. Of course every man should consider all things in the light of Christ.

But other men have many obligations imposed on them by the immanent logic of their professions, whether it be that of doctor, statesman, professor, artist, worker, etc. Then there are the specific duties of the husband, the father, the wife, the mother, etc. Here, too, everything should be seen in the light of Christ and from the point of view of our eternal destination. This point of view should always have priority over various specific duties rooted in the immanent logic of things, according to the words of Christ: "And if your right hand is an occasion of sin to you, cut it off and cast it from you; for it is better for you that one of your members should be lost than that your whole body should go into hell" (Mt. 5, 30). And all the duties rooted in the immanent logic of things must be transformed in Christ and be transfigured by him. But for the priest the immanent logic of his office is identical with the "one thing necessary."

In speaking of the immanent logic (*Eigengesetzlichkeit*) of things one usually refers to the laws flowing from the logic or neutral structure of some thing or some activity. Thus one cannot really speak of a moral or religious immanent logic, for here we are not just dealing with the neutral laws which are otherwise always present. All these neutral laws are merely hypothetical in nature (*if* you want to do something, *then* you have to observe certain laws). Here we want to say that the priesthood has no immanent logic analogous to what we find in the doctor, the scientist, the merchant, and even the husband and the father. The theme of the priest's office is identical with the religious theme. The raison d'être of the existence of the priest, as of every Christian, is to glorify God by being transformed in Christ. But his office of serving the Church and glorifying God by offering the holy Mass, administering the sacraments, and proclaiming the the word of God — is so intimately bound up with the primary theme of every Christian's life that this office has no immanent logic, for it has nothing not belonging to the sphere of the absolute, of the supernatural.

Right and wrong appeals to the primitive Church

We must also point out that it would be false to argue from the fact that priestly celibacy was not obligatory in the primitive church, to the fact that celibacy is not better and is not more adequate to the office of the priest. However justified it is to want to return to the spirit, the ardor, and the strength of faith in the early Church and to take as one's model the attitude of the apostles — still, when it comes to institutional things such as the value and adequacy of some prescription regarding an office, an appeal to the state of things in the beginning is no argument.

In the Church we not only find that the faith which implicitly embraces the true revelation of Christ develops to explicit dogmatic formulations; we also find an unfolding of the original spirit in the differentiation of Canon Law. Thus the decisive question is not *when* something was introduced in the course of the Church's history, but rather whether it accords with the spirit of the early Church, whether it is an organic expression of the spirit of Christ in the domain of the Church's formal structure, whether it better corresponds to the nature of the Church.

Is celibacy imposed from without upon the priest in the Western Church, simply for historical reasons — or is it something which deeply accords with the priesthood, so that it is an organic result of the spirit of the priesthood — that is the decisive question. Is celibacy as such more adequate for the priest, is it the meaningful consequence of the priesthood? Does it have a great value? Is it objectively more desirable when priests do not marry?

The objections of Wendelin Kellner to obligatory celibacy clearly betray an approach in which a sense for the supernatural has been completely lost. To say that the evangelical counsels are only aspects of community living shows that the sublime importance of consecrated virginity has been utterly misunderstood. It is thoroughly false to say that only life in community makes it meaningful to remain unmarried. Here is a complete unawareness of the depth and importance of the sensual sphere on the one hand, and of the mystery of total self-donation to Christ on the other. Here one forgets or treats as outdated

all the sublime words of the Church fathers on consecrated virginity, as well as everything which filled
the souls of countless saints and other priests and
religious as they elected to live in consecrated abstinence.[3]

NOTES

1. Cf. Wendelin Kellner, "Priesterlicher Zoelibat ohne Gemeinschaft?" in *Der Zoelibat* (Gruenewaldreihe, 1968, edited
by Franz Boekle).

2. I want to quote here a passage from a moving letter
which a deeply devout man wrote me after hearing a lecture
of mine on celibacy. This man has been completely crippled
for 40 years and was brought, to my lectures on a stretcher
from his home 80 miles away:

"I was confined to bed for years because of an accident,
and I would have never found peace of soul, which can
dwell even in a broken body, but for the unrelenting efforts
and sacrifices of a certain priest. One day in visiting me he
spoke to me for a long time about how I should follow
Christ by offering up my sufferings with Him to the Father,
and how happy this would make me. I dare not think what
would have become of me if at this moment the priest, at
the sound of a car horn, had gotten up and said: 'I'll try
to come back next weekend, but I've promised my wife and
children a picnic and they're waiting for me downstairs in
the car.' "

3. Closely related to the failure to understand the value
of consecrated celibacy is the failure to understand the
I-Thou communion with Christ. It is a typical exclusion of
all of supernatural reality. This is also revealed in the
arbitrary identification of obeying and serving. The passage
in Mt. 20, 26, "Whoever wishes to become great among you
shall be your servant," refers primarily to the humility
actualized in serving. Serving is certainly an expression of
love. But here, where Christ emphasizes the contrast between

the great in the world who rule, and the great in the Kingdom of God, it is humiliation and humility which stand in
the foreground. This has nothing to do with obedience.
Obedience is always submission to an authority. The servant
of course obeys the master — but the master who, like
Christ in washing the feet of the apostles, serves in humility,
is not obeying anyone. Humbly serving others does not imply
any obedience toward them, rather we obey always and exclusively the God-man Christ.

The height of this confusion is reached when Kellner says:
what the Gospel demands of the disciples is community! The
inexhaustible wealth of supernatural virtues implied by the
imitation of Christ is here reduced to community, community
is identified with love even on a natural level, and the unique
community rooted in Christ is confused with community in
general.

Chapter VIII

The Unmarried State of the Priest and Human Love

Some of those advocating the abolition of celibacy contend that a priest in being married would, through his devotion first to his wife and then to his children, learn a devotion to other men which would enable him to be warmer and more understanding in dealing with souls as a priest. This argument not only claims that remaining unmarried easily leads to the egoism typical of the bachelor, it also claims that the lack of experience that comes from not loving a wife makes the life of the priest poorer, colder, his heart harder.

Misunderstanding of supernatural love

This argument is a typical expression of a thoroughly secularized mentality and of a complete misunderstanding of the nature of charity. Those who argue like this have forgotten that charity, which is distinguished from all forms of natural love as something qualitatively completely new — and even more from all humanitarian "love of neighbor" — can and must be achieved only in a personal act of love for God in Christ. Only Christ can, in a full I-Thou communion with the individual soul, melt our hearts and fill them with that holy goodness with which we approach our neighbor in love, in that holy love of which St. Paul speaks so wonderfully in Chapter 13 of the first letter to the Corinthians.

The degree of the warmth and devotion of the priest depends exclusively on how deep and living his love for Christ is. No natural human love, however great — though it can have a great and morally elevating influence — can ever inflame in our hearts charity for our neighbor.

Celibacy for the love of Christ and bachelorhood

A second great error at the basis of this argument is that it overlooks the abyss which separates remaining unmarried for the sake of the kingdom of heaven, from remaining unmarried by accident or even because of the egoism typical of a certain kind of bachelor. We have already expressly referred to this distinction. We have seen how wonderfully the celibate or the person living in consecrated virginity or abstinence manifests his faith in Christ and his love for him. Now we have to emphasize that this radical difference is clearly not seen by those who think that the priest's ability to devote himself to souls will be increased by his being married.

In other writings I have often mentioned that charity, deep love of neighbor, concern for the ultimate welfare of souls, for their sanctification and eternal salvation, can be much greater in a hermit than in a priest who is secretary of a Catholic welfare organization. The hermit shows his charity in prayer; but it should be clear for every believing Catholic that this prayer is not only a highly important actualization of this holy love but that it is also a greatly effective help for those for whom he prays.

This of course in no way means that the hermit is a model for the pastor. To be a hermit or to belong to an order like the Carthusians is a great and wonderful vocation, but a rare vocation, one sui generis. We only mention the hermit to show how charity can express itself in very different ways, according to one's calling, and that the degree of one's charity depends exclusively on the degree of one's love for Christ and one's transformation in Christ.

The danger of the priest becoming cold of heart: The roots of this danger and its cure

When the personal communion of love with Christ is not fully developed, then of course the relation of the priest to the souls entrusted to him can take on the character of a cold fulfilment of duty and can even lead to a certain hardness of heart.

This is a typical secularization of the priesthood,

which is no longer seen in its supernatural, sacral character. That is really a legalistic perversion; here the priest tends to become a mere employee.

To overcome this hardening of the heart a deep friendship can be a great help, such as that of St. Augustine with Nebridius, Alypius, and St. Paulinus of Nola, or such as the deep love of Don Bosco for his mother, or the love of St. Bernard for his brother. It may be that a deep natural (as distinguished from supernatural) friendship can awaken the heart of such a priest from its "sleep," or can prevent this hardening of the heart from ever occurring. But such a friendship, such a natural love can never be the basis for a greater love of souls, for a greater understanding of them, a greater devotion to them. The natural friendship, if it awakens the heart, can only lead to a deeper relation to Christ — and only the deeper love of Christ can bestow new warmth on one's charity, one's love for souls, one's priestly devotion to them, indeed, can give "wings" to one's charity. Natural love for another, being good to him, can never directly fill the soul with holy goodness for every potential neighbor. The natural love can only, with the help of God, be an instrument for awakening the soul and of leading it to a new conversion to Christ. Deep devotion to souls, pastoral warmth, holy zeal for their sanctification and salvation, can only issue from a direct relation to Christ, from love for Jesus. All the saints give us an example of this.

But this possible awakening of the soul does not presuppose marriage. Every love, every deep attachment to another person or bond with him can fulfill this function — neither marital love nor marriage is necessary. Celibacy, or being unmarried for the sake of the kingdom of heaven, is not responsible for this hardening of the heart, nor would marriage as such be a guarantee against this hardening. In how many marriages does the husband remain an egoist, does he remain so consumed by his profession that his heart increasingly "goes to sleep," becomes cold!

One cannot even say that the priest is exposed to the danger of hardening when he has never had a special love for another person — let us suppose that his parents died when he was young or that they showed him so little love that he never had an affectionate relation to them, and let us suppose that later in life he never found persons who were his close friends, and that he then feels a calling to the priesthood and to celibacy for the sake of the kingdom of heaven. No; if a burning love for Jesus lives in his soul, if Christ has melted his heart, then he does not at all fall into this hardening.[1] The one thing that we have to emphasize is that deep friendships — of course ones that are transformed by Jesus, holy friendships — are in no way an obstacle for the priest's full devotion to souls. As we saw earlier, one does not renounce such friendships in accepting celibacy.

So we see how insensitive to certain realities and how perverse is the statement that marriage would teach the priest true devotion, that it would enable his relation to souls to become warmer, livelier, more understanding.

NOTES

1. "The priest should apply himself above all else to developing, with all the love which grace inspires in him, his close relationship with Christ, and to meditating on the inexhaustible and blessed mystery of Christ; he should also acquire an ever deeper sense of the mystery of the Church. There would be the risk of his state of life seeming pointless and unfounded if seen apart from this mystery.

"Priestly piety, nourished at the table of God's Word and the Holy Eucharist, lived within the cycle of the liturgical year, inspired by a warm and trusting devotion to the blessed Virgin, the Mother of the Supreme and Eternal High Priest and Queen of the Apostles, will bring him to the source of a true spiritual life which alone provides a solid foundation for the observance of celibacy." "On Priestly Celibacy," para. 75.

Chapter IX

The "Institutional" Church and the Church of Love

Revolt against the institutional Church goes hand in hand with the struggle against obligatory celibacy. The antipathy for the so-called "institutional Church" is expressed in the attempt to replace authoritative formal obligations by voluntary bonds.

Formal and material communities

An important distinction in the realm of relations among men and in the realm of communities is the distinction between material and formal. Material and formal have here a meaning analogous to their meaning in the distinction between material and formal ethics. "Material" here clearly has nothing to do with matter or physical bodies.[1] It rather refers to qualitative fullness, to wealth of content, as opposed to that which is poor in content but has sharp contours, to that which is meant by the word "formal."

The relation of an employer to his employees is a formal relation, the relation between two friends is material. The formal relation is established by social acts (such as the promise, contracts of all kinds), whereas the material relation grows out of mutual respect and love.

In our context we are mainly interested in the difference between material and formal communities.

An association is a purely formal community, a circle of friends is a purely material one. The association has a juridical aspect and is even rooted in a special way in the world of legal things. It is established by a social act of two or more persons. It has certain rules which define its purpose, its structure, and the competence of its president and other officers. One also enters the association by a social act. Whether the members of the association are friends with one another or not, has no bearing on the reality of this community. It suffices that they have entered the association, that they share its purpose, and observe its rules.

A circle of friends is clearly distinguished from this purely formal community. It has as such no juridical aspect, it is not a legal thing. It does not have the clearly demarcated form of an association. But it is a much deeper, richer community. Its principle of unity is the basic convictions of its members, the positions which they personally take toward things; it is their mutual sympathy, respect, and love which bind them together. The circle of friends is not established by social acts, it is not founded at a certain moment, but rather develops organically in the coming together of men who understand one another, who are bound together by common interests of an intellectual and spiritual kind, and who gradually draw closer to one another. There is no president here, though a striking personality can occupy a place of prominence among the friends.

A person cannot enter a circle of friends by a social act, he rather grows into it by being attracted by the spiritual atmosphere of the circle and by the individual persons who belong to it and who accept him with sympathy, respect, and love.

But the difference between formal and material communities is not always so strikingly given as in the cases just mentioned. There are formal communities possessing more depth and content than an association, for example the state. The state is nevertheless a formal community in comparison with a nation, which is a material, cultural community. When both embrace the same people, when for instance a state embraces a whole nation and only this nation, then we have an intimate union of the two, though this union does not efface the fundamental difference between the material and the formal communities. Finally there are communities possessing both a material and a formal character, such as marriage and the family.[2]

Communities which are both material and formal

But there are material communities which by their

very nature require an adequate form. Or as we can say more concretely, there is a type of community to whose nature it belongs to be both a material and a formal community. Nor are the material and formal elements merely juxtaposed, they rather form an organic whole. This holds for the family: this material communion of love requires a clear external form which includes a juridical aspect.

There are two things to be understood here:

First, the value of the formal aspect of a community. This formal aspect possesses a high value in itself and is not something merely utilitarian. In the case of an association the value of the formal element is quite modest. But when we think of the clear, sharply demarcated structure of a state, the dignity of the formal element is clearly revealed — in the laws of the state, in its order, and in its structure which serves justice, security, and the common good. What an evil is anarchy!

Secondly, the value of the organic interpenetration in a community of the formal and material aspects. We have to see that it is a particular perfection of a community when it is at once a material and a formal community, when the material and formal elements interpenetrate, when the formal element is the adequate form required by the meaning of the material community. This is seen in the highest natural community, in marriage. The social act of the consensus in marrying is an expression of marital love. Marital love necessarily reaches out for a solemn formal bond. The formal element is not inorganically attached to the communion of love in marriage but is rather necessarily intended by this love and grows organically out of it.

The same holds for a religious order. But in the holy Church the interpenetration of material and formal community reaches a climax. The visible Church, its hierarchic structure, Canon Law all belong necessarily to the mystical body of Christ on earth. The formal element of the Church is found even among the apostles and especially in Peter's elevation to head of the Church. Only a hopeless metaphysical Bohemian could take scandal at the institutional character of the Church and could confuse the glorious form of the Church which is marked with the spirit of the supernatural, with worldly institutions. The difference between the Church and all natural communities does not lie in the fact that the Church has no external form but rather in the fact that its external form is of supernatural origin.

The danger of institutionalism and legalism

All mistakes and imperfections of those who held the offices of the Church, for instance the legalism with which many reproach the "institutional" Church, do not result from the Church being not only a "church of love" but also a "church of law," from the Church being (as one used to put it) not

only Johannine but also Petrine; they rather result
from the imperfections of the persons who held these
offices. If there was legalism in the Church, this re-
sulted from the secularized mentality of those who
ruled the institutional Church like any other purely
natural formal community, such as the state. But
even the state is not necessarily legalistic. Legalism
is not a characteristic of any kind of community but
rather of the attitude of the person who holds an
office in a bureaucratic spirit, who clings to the letter and ignores the spirit. In the case of the legalism
of the Church there is also this, that the decisive difference between natural and supernatural communities is not taken into account. Legalism here is always a result of secularization. We have only to
think of the many Popes who were saints, such as
Gregory I, to grasp the full glory of the "institutional"
church. This Pope permeated the holy Church in its
formal structure with the spirit of Christ. So we see
what an important new aspect of the realization of
the mystical body of Christ on earth, is represented
by the institutional Church. We understand how a
clear, juridically demarcated form — which even in
natural communities always has a certain value in
itself — takes on a unique value when it is the
"outer side" of the holy Church, the bride of Christ;
how this "outer side" of the Church is a basically
new way in which the supernatural breaks into this
world. The so-called "Johannine" church is in reality

a vague concept, which, characteristically enough, keeps recurring as the ideal of certain heretics such as Joachim of Flora. Whoever truly loves the Church and understands her supernatural character, also loves the "institutional Church," he grasps the great gift which it represents, for him the working of the Holy Ghost shines forth from this formal structure, from the existence of Canon Law.

Let a person once understand, on the one hand, how the mystical body of Christ is deeply and indissolubly bound up with the blessedness and greatness of the holy "form" of the visible church, and on the other hand, how radically this form differs from all merely natural formal communities; then he must also see how the greatness of the priesthood necessarily presupposes the formal structure of the holy Church, and how all attempts to free the priesthood from its roots in Church law, ultimately lead to a destruction of the nature of the priesthood.

NOTES

1. In German one distinguishes between *material* (the specific antithesis to formal) and *materiell* (of or pertaining to matter and physical bodies). In English we have only the word material to embrace both meanings.

2. Cf. my *Metaphysik der Gemeinschaft* (Josef Habbel Verlag, Regensburg, 1955), Part II, Chap. V, pp. 207-220.

Chapter X
Conclusion

We saw that abstinence for the sake of the kingdom of heaven, the celibacy of the priest, is a unique manifestation of faith and of love for Christ. The same is true of the priesthood. In reflecting on this we see how impossible it is to consider celibacy from a purely natural point of view and to exclude the element of God's grace. If one only emphasizes various psychological factors, the difficulty of living in abstinence, the struggle against sexual temptations, possible bitterness and hardening of heart, and fails to mention the special grace which God gives those who dedicate themselves to him in this heroic way, then one distorts the real situation.[1] For if we exclude the element of God's grace, of the help which he grants to those who elect to live in abstinence or to remain unmarried for the sake of the kingdom of heaven, then we let go of the presupposition for choosing the priesthood. For the priesthood loses all its meaning when I see the world and man's life in a purely natural light, when I take no account of the existence of an almighty God, of his infinite love and mercy for us. Then the calling of God to the priesthood becomes an illusion. If someone really regards this calling as a reality, then he has to take account of the help and grace of God which will help him to fulfill what this state of life requires of him. Otherwise how could he dare to be ordained and to take upon himself all the great responsibility of this sacred and high office? And the same holds for the calling to celibacy. Here too the calling of God cannot be separated from faith in the special grace which God gives those whom he calls to this state.

And the deep affinity between priesthood and celibacy can only be understood by him who counts on the grace of God, on the divine assistance, which is an indispensable condition for both priesthood and celibacy.

For those who forget this decisive element the priesthood becomes one profession among others, like that of the doctor, the teacher, the researcher. The calling to the priesthood is reduced to the interest and attraction which the priesthood has for them. They conceive the priest more as a benefactor of men than as a sacred servant of God and his holy Church in its primary work of glorifying God and striving to secure the eternal salvation of men. As soon as one takes up this secularized view of the priesthood and looks upon celibacy only as unnecessary ballast, one has lost the condition for truly understanding the priesthood, celibacy, and the relation between them.

Pope John XXIII said: "It deeply hurts us that . . . anyone can dream that the Church is planning or thinks it appropriate to renounce the law of ecclesiastical celibacy which has been from time immemorial and still remains one of the purest and noblest glories of priesthood. The law of ecclesiastical celibacy and the efforts necessary to preserve it always recall to mind the struggles of the heroic times when the Church of Christ had to fight for and succeeded in obtaining her threefold glory; for celibacy is the sign of the victory of the Christ's church, employing all her strength, to be free, chaste, and catholic."[2]

We want to close our reflections on celibacy by profoundly thanking our Holy Father Pope Paul VI for preserving obligatory celibacy despite all the vehement attempts to abolish this holy tradition.

The following words of our Holy Father must fill with deep joy and gratitude every Catholic who truly loves the holy Church and understands her character as a supernatural institution:

"Hence we consider that the present law of celibacy should today continue to be firmly linked to the sacerdotal office. This law should support the minister in his exclusive, definitive and total choice of the unique and supreme love of Christ; it should uphold him in the entire dedication of himself to the public worship of God and to the service of the Church; it should characterize his state of life both among the faithful and in the world at large."[3]

NOTES

1. "The Church cannot and should not forget that the choice of celibacy — provided that it is made with human and Christian prudence and responsibility — is governed by grace which, far from destroying or doing violence to nature, elevates it and imparts to it supernatural powers and vigor. God, who has created and redeemed man, knows what He can ask of him and gives him everything necessary to be able to do what his Creator and Redeemer asks of him. St. Augustine, who had fully and painfully experienced in himself the nature of man, exclaimed: 'Grant what You command, and command what You will.' " "On Priestly Celibacy," para. 51.

2. Pope John XXIII, Second Allocution to the Roman Synod, Jan. 26, 1960, quoted by Pope Paul VI, "On Priestly Celibacy," para. 37.

3. "On Priestly Celibacy," para. 14.